fantastic
party cakes

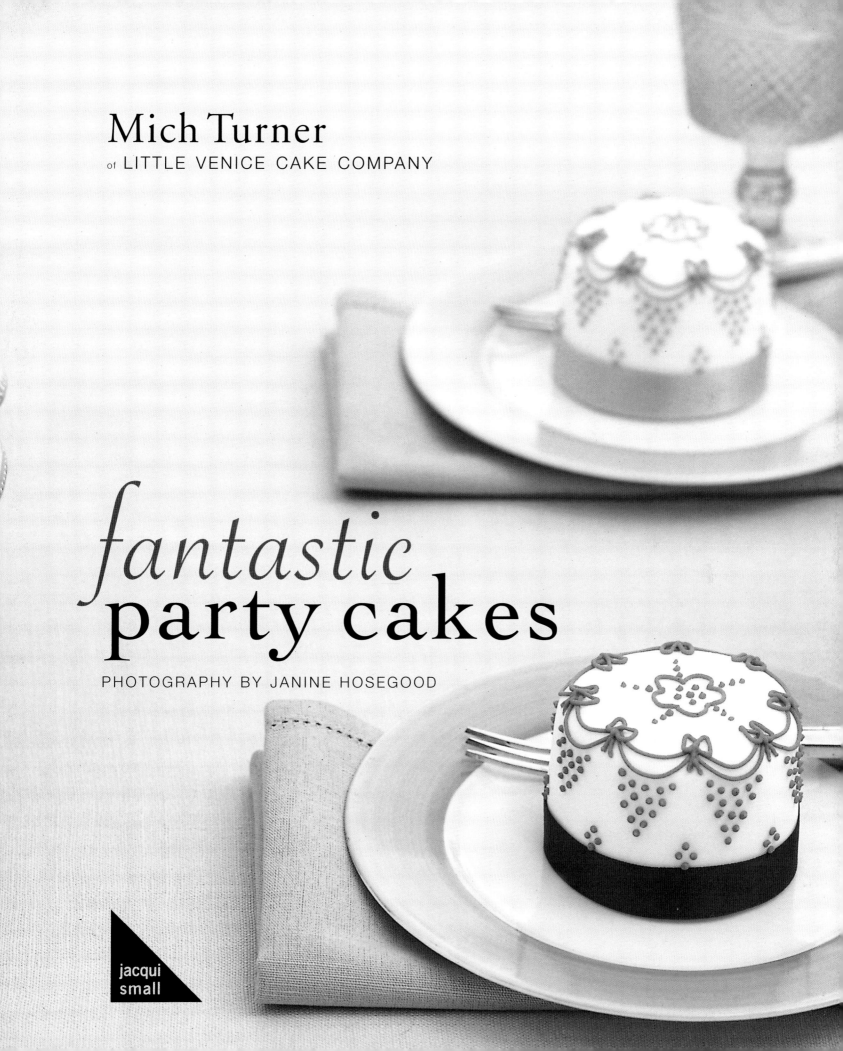

Mich Turner
of LITTLE VENICE CAKE COMPANY

fantastic party cakes

PHOTOGRAPHY BY JANINE HOSEGOOD

jacqui
small

I dedicate this book to my boys –
Phil, Marlow and George.
With Love Forever.

First published in 2007 by Jacqui Small LLP
an imprint of Aurum Press Ltd
7 Greenland Street
London NW1 0ND

Text copyright © Mich Turner

Photography, design and layout copyright
© Jacqui Small 2007

Publisher Jacqui Small
Editorial Managers Kate John and Judith Hannam
Editor Madeline Weston
Designers Maggie Town and Beverly Price
Photographer Janine Hosegood
Production Peter Colley

A catalogue record for this book is available from
the British Library.

ISBN-10: 1 903221 89 7
ISBN-13: 978 1 903221 89 1

2010 2009 2008 2007

10 9 8 7 6 5 4 3 2 1

Printed in China

contents

introduction Welcome to my second book showcasing a collection of *Fantastic Party Cakes*. A fantastic party requires a fantastic cake and this book will provide ideas for every occasion. In the chapter *Delicious Treats*, I have included a range of gorgeous base-cake recipes which can be enjoyed in their own right for a special weekend afternoon tea. Alternatively, they can be used in the first two chapters for bite-size iced and chocolate cakes for summer banquets, Christmas canapé parties and baby showers, or small party cakes for more formal occasions including weddings, anniversaries, birthdays and Christmas. You also will find a mouthwatering selection of fluffy desserts to choose from for lunch and dinner parties including cheesecakes, roulades and meringues. I finish with a collection of beautifully hand-decorated pastries and cookies which make fabulous gifts or table settings.

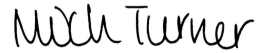

decorated delights

decorated delights There is something rather endearing about these individually covered or decorated cakes and bites. These beautiful designs are very special as they have 'just for me' appeal. Befitting any celebration, they are sure to be a talking point or a lasting reminder of a fantastic party. I have created these designs using the recipes featured in the chapter *Delicious Treats*. Bake the cakes in a square tin for ease of stamping out rounds or cutting out squares. A single layer 20cm square cake will yield 16 individual 5cm round or square cakes or 25 x 4cm canapé-sized cakes.

chocolate boxes

These gorgeous little chocolate boxes are a very sophisticated way of serving a delicious chocolate-almond torte, sandwiched with espresso buttercream. They work equally well in white or milk chocolate. Cut into a perfect cube then surround it with tempered chocolate panels, and finish with an organza ribbon and a pretty label.

you will need

5cm cube cakes covered in chocolate or espresso buttercream

dark chocolate – allow 150g per cake

sharp knife

organza ribbon 15mm wide – allow 50cm per cake

pretty cards

method

1 Temper the dark chocolate as shown in the techniques on page 147. Spread the chocolate out on to a marble slab or stainless steel tray to a depth of 2–3mm. Once the chocolate has just set, use the templates on page 153 to cut out 2 short sides, 2 long sides and 1 lid for each cake.

2 Fix the 2 short sides first on to opposite sides of one cake – they should adhere to the buttercream. Then fix the 2 longer sides on the two remaining sides before applying the lid.

3 Starting with the centre of the ribbon in the centre of the lid, wrap up the cake and tie the ribbon, fixing the pretty card into place. Finish all the cakes in the same way.

4 Serve on square plates. These cakes will keep for a few days once completed as they are shelf stable.

tip

These cakes are quite difficult to handle – try this size first before attempting to make them any smaller. A collection of 3 cubes in white, milk and dark chocolate can make a stunning gift presented in a box.

marbled chocolate truffles

I first served these decadent and scrumptious marbled chocolate truffles at the launch of my first book, *Spectacular Cakes*. They proved such a success with the guests that I knew should feature in the second book. Use a combination of cake flavours such as banana butterscotch (page 85), chocolate almond (page 90) or chocca mocca pecan (page 95) with marbled chocolates for a special canapé party.

you will need

4cm round cakes

chocolate scrolls and fans decoration

white chocolate plastique (first coat) – allow 40g per cake

white, milk or dark chocolate (top coat) – allow 60g per cake

fork

method

1 Make the chocolate decorations following the technique on page 147. Cover the 4cm round cakes with an initial coat of white chocolate plastique as shown in the techniques on page 149 .

2 In 3 separate bowls, temper white, milk and dark chocolate. Set the cakes on a wire rack with a sheet of non-stick greaseproof paper underneath. Using a large metal spoon or small ladle, spoon tempered chocolate over the cakes until fully covered as shown. Gently tap the rack to settle the chocolate.

3 Before the chocolate sets, dip a fork in a contrasting chocolate and marble over the cake creating interesting swirls as shown. Once the chocolate begins to set, decorate the top of each truffle with a chocolate decoration. Allow the cakes to set before using a palette knife to transfer the cakes to a serving plate.

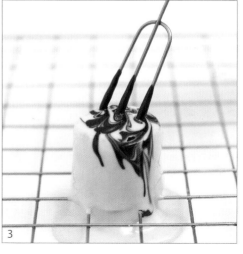

white chocolate pearls

These white-chocolate covered decorated cakes are charmingly chic for a wedding buffet. They look good presented on a large cake stand and served, one per guest, for dessert. They also make perfect take-home wedding favours presented in clear plastic boxes.

you will need

5cm square cakes

white chocolate plastique – allow 165g per cake for 2 coats and a fan

icing sugar, for dusting

small rolling pin

piping bag

tempered white chocolate for the pearls

cream grosgrain ribbon 15mm wide – allow 20cm per cake

method

1 Lightly knead the white chocolate plastique on a work surface dusted with icing sugar. Roll out a 6cm square very thinly and gently mould it into a fan shape as shown; pinch the base and trim it with a sharp knife. Make one for each cake (the picture on the right shows two fans on the cake).

2 Cover each 5cm square cake with an initial covering of white chocolate plastique followed by a top coat as shown in the techniques on page 149.

3 Fill a piping bag with a small amount of cooled tempered white chocolate. Snip the end of the piping bag. Fix a length of cream grosgrain ribbon around the base of each cake and pipe random 'pearls' over the top and sides. Fix the fans into position on the top of each cake.

fondant diamonds

Fondant-covered cup cakes have become increasingly popular and these sophisticated designs would grace the smartest party; they are suitable for bridal showers, wedding buffets and adult birthdays. Use a light base such as the vanilla cake (page 83) or lime and coconut (page 80) without the buttercream as the fondant icing is very sweet.

you will need

5cm round cakes

fondant icing – allow 75g per cake

pink and brown edible food colours

marzipan – allow 60g per cake

6cm silver cup cake cases

ribbon or elastic bands to hold the cases in position

2 piping bags

2 no. 1.5 nozzles

royal icing for the top design

method

1 Make the fondant icing (see page 144) and colour half with pink and half with brown edible colouring. Cover the 5cm round cakes first with marzipan and then coloured fondant icing as shown in the techniques (pages 141 and 144). Place each fondant-covered cup cake in a silver case and hold in position with a tied length of plain ribbon or an elastic band until set.

2 Colour some royal icing and fill a piping bag with a no. 1.5 nozzle and the royal icing (use pink on brown cakes and vice versa). Using the template on page 153 as a guide, pipe the design freehand on to the top of each cup cake. Allow to set. Remove the ribbon or elastic band prior to serving.

2

monochrome lace

This design was inspired by lace from a Pearl Lowe collection. It is particularly striking in black and white and has become a firm favourite with clients of Little Venice Cake Company.

you will need

5cm round cakes

marzipan – allow 60g per cake

white sugar paste – allow 75g per cake

black ribbon 9mm wide – allow 15cm per cake

greaseproof paper

scribe

royal icing

black edible food colour

piping bag

no. 1.5 nozzle

method

1 Cover the 5cm round cakes with marzipan and sugar paste as shown in the techniques on pages 141 and 143. Fix a length of black ribbon around the base of each cake. Trace the template from page 156 on to greaseproof paper and, placing the tracing over each cake in turn, scribe the centre flower and the middle of the ribbon bows on to the top of each cake using the scribe.

2 Colour some royal icing with black edible colouring. Fill a piping bag with a no. 1.5 nozzle and the black icing. Pipe the detail on to the cake as shown, adding the pearls underneath the scrolls and around the base ribbon.

tip

This design transposes well in a variety of colours – change the colours to complement your party.

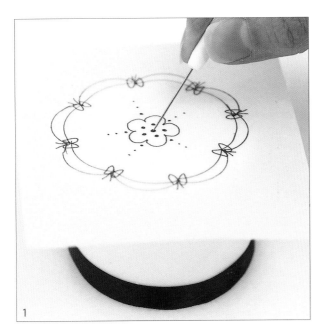

bollywood

These stylish Bollywood designs are bold, bright and very up to date – and such fun. The vibrant colours of saffron, lime, tangerine and fuchsia look particularly effective when they are clustered en masse.

you will need

5cm round cakes

marzipan – allow 60g per cake

yellow, orange, fuchsia and lime coloured sugar paste – allow 75g per cake

gold ribbon 9mm wide – allow 15cm per cake

greaseproof paper

scribe

royal icing

old gold edible food colour

piping bag

no. 1.5 nozzle

gold dust

dipping alcohol

fine paintbrush

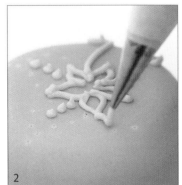

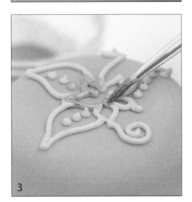

method

1 Cover the 5cm round cakes with marzipan and coloured sugar paste as shown in the techniques on pages 141 and 143. Fix a length of gold ribbon around the base of each cake. Trace the two templates from page 152 on to greaseproof paper. Scribe one of the two designs on to the top of each cake using the scribe and the traced template.

2 Colour some royal icing with old gold food colouring. Fill a piping bag with a no. 1.5 nozzle and old gold royal icing. Pipe the detail on to each cake as shown, adding the pearls, swirls and flowers. Allow to set for at least 2 hours.

3 Dissolve a small amount of gold dust in dipping alcohol and brush on to the Bollywood design using a fine paintbrush.

pretty posies

Delicately hand-piped flowers and leaves are very effective decoration for these little cakes. They look particularly impressive in all white for weddings; I recreated this design in shades of pink on a larger cake for my God-daughter Imogen's christening.

you will need

5cm round cakes

marzipan – allow 60g per cake

ivory sugar paste – allow 75g per cake

sage green ribbon 15mm wide – allow 15cm per cake

royal icing

purple, pink and green edible food colours

3 piping bags

2 no. 1.5 nozzles

method

1 Cover the 5cm round cakes with marzipan and sugar paste as shown in the techniques on pages 141 and 143. Fix a length of sage green ribbon around the base of each cake. Colour some royal icing with the three edible food colours. Fill a piping bag with no. 1.5 nozzle and purple royal icing. Pipe a circle of petals on the cake – trailing the petal to the centre of each flower. Repeat over the top and sides of the cake in different sizes as shown.

2 Fill a second piping bag with no. 1.5 nozzle and pink royal icing. Pipe a second row of petals inside the first coming to a point in the centre of each flower.

3 Fill a third piping bag with green royal icing and snip the end of the bag to form a small 'V' (as shown in techniques for fondant red roses on page 41). Pressure pipe green leaves to frame the flowers as shown.

coconut butterflies

I made these coconut rounds out of the lime and coconut cake (page 80) but other flavours would work equally well. The sugar discs can be made in advance and you can use any colours to suit the celebration. These pretty little cakes are just right for a female birthday party.

you will need

5cm round sugar paste discs – allow 15g per cake

icing sugar, for dusting

greaseproof paper

scribe

3 piping bags

no. 1.5, no. 2 and large star nozzles

royal icing for piping and flooding the butterflies

edible food colours of your choice

paintbrush

5cm round cakes

palette knife

buttercream – choose from vanilla, orange, lemon curd and chocolate flavours (pages 138–9) – allow 30g per cake

toasted coconut – allow 10g per cake

method

1 Prepare the icing discs: roll out the white sugar paste to a depth of 3mm and stamp out 5cm rounds. Place on a board or tray well dusted with icing sugar and allow to dry overnight. Trace the butterfly template on page 152 on to greaseproof paper and scribe this on to each of the sugar discs. Fill a piping bag with a no. 2 nozzle and coloured royal icing. Pipe the outline of the butterfly as shown. Fill a separate piping bag with another coloured flooding icing and snip the end. Flood the wings of the butterflies as shown.

2 Use a paintbrush to carefully pull the icing to all corners of the wings. Allow to skin over for 20 minutes before decorating.

3 Fill a piping bag with a no. 1.5 nozzle and the original coloured royal icing. Pipe a 5-pointed flower on the top of both wings of each butterfly and 4 pearls on the lower wings. Allow to set overnight or at least 6 hours.

4 Cut out the individual round cakes – it helps if the cake is chilled for 30 minutes – and use a palette knife to smooth a small amount of buttercream over the sides. Roll the cakes in the toasted coconut and set aside.

5 Fill a piping bag with a large star nozzle and fresh buttercream. Pipe a swirl of buttercream on the top of each cake and position a sugar butterfly disc at an angle on the top. Present the cakes together on a pretty cake stand.

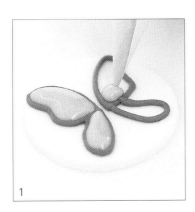

bugs and butterflies

These elaborate individually hand-painted cakes would look stunning individually boxed and ribboned and presented as wedding favours. The colours can be changed to suit any occasion. The technique is quite time consuming, so use a cake base with a good shelf life – such as the sticky date (page 86) or banana butterscotch cake (page 85).

you will need

5cm round cakes

marzipan – allow 60g per cake

caramel sugar paste – allow 75g per cake

berry-coloured ribbon 15mm wide – allow 15cm per cake

royal icing to fix ribbon in position

greaseproof paper

scribe

cocoa butter

various colour dusts

paintbrushes

method

1 Cover the 5cm round cakes with marzipan and sugar paste as shown in the techniques on pages 141 and 143. Fix a length of berry-coloured ribbon around the base of each cake with a little royal icing. Trace a range of designs from the templates on page 152 on to greaseproof paper. Scribe these on to the cakes using a scribe. Use different bugs and butterflies in different positions for a truly individual collection.

2 Melt a small piece of cocoa butter on a small saucer over a cup of hot water. Blend the cocoa butter with a colour dust and paint the traced designs on to each cake. Build up the colour and intensity by adding more layers. Finish by adding fine black detail to each bug for their limbs, antennae and pincers.

tip

If the cocoa butter starts to solidify, replace the water in the cup underneath the saucer with freshly boiled water.

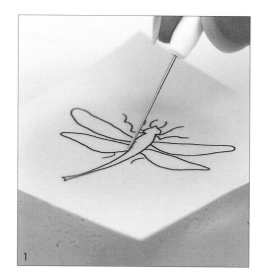

christmas canapé collection

When we invite our neighbours in for champagne, carols and festive treats at Christmas, these chic cakes are perfect – hand decorated with seasonal designs and brushed with gold – and boxed they make a lovely gift. I recommend the chocolate almond (page 90), sticky date (page 86), or chocca mocca pecan cake (page 95) for inclusion inside.

you will need

5cm square cakes

white chocolate plastique – allow 70g per cake

dark chocolate plastique – allow 85g per cake

petal paste coloured with old gold – allow 5g for 3 holly leaves for 1 cake

small rolling pin

small holly veiner/plunger-cutter (2cm)

new kitchen sponge

1 quantity royal icing (page 145)

old gold edible food colour

gold ribbon 15mm wide – allow 20cm per cake

greaseproof paper

scribe

piping bag

no. 1.5 nozzle

gold lustre

dipping alcohol

fine paintbrush

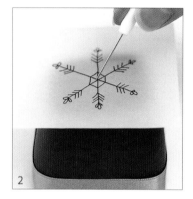
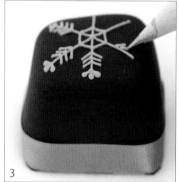

method

1 Cover each 5cm square cake with an initial covering of white chocolate plastique followed by a top coat of dark chocolate plastique as shown in the techniques on page 149. Roll out the coloured petal paste (page 141) very finely and vein and cut out holly leaves. Allow to dry on a soft sponge to create interesting shapes.

2 Colour the royal icing with old gold colouring. Fix a length of gold ribbon around the base of each cake with a little royal icing. Trace the snowflake design on page 154 on to greaseproof paper and scribe the design through on to the top of one cake. Repeat with one third the total number of cakes.

3 Fill a piping bag with a no. 1.5 nozzle and old gold royal icing. Hand pipe the snowflake design following the template. Hand pipe random Christmas trees on the sides of another third of the cakes as shown. Place 3 holly leaves on top of each of the remaining cakes and hand pipe berries in the centre.

4 Suspend a small amount of gold lustre in dipping alcohol in a small bowl. Brush the gold lustre liquid carefully over the designs ensuring the holly leaves are well covered and painting in stars at the top of some of the Christmas trees. Present on a gold plate or Christmas platter or in clear boxes tied with gold ribbon.

polka swirl hearts

These bright, vibrant cakes look stunning on a tiered cake stand. Change the colours to suit the occasion. They were originally commissioned for a Valentine's Day promotion held at London's famous Fortnum & Mason but have now become a firm favourite at Little Venice Cake Company.

you will need

5cm square cakes

marzipan – allow 70g per cake

white sugar paste – allow 85g per cake

party ribbon 9mm wide – allow 20cm per cake

royal icing, to fix the ribbon in position and add the swirls on to the hearts

small rolling pin

various coloured sugar pastes

heart plunger-cutter

sugar glue

edible food colour of choice

piping bag

no. 1.5 nozzle

method

1 Cover the cakes with marzipan and sugar paste following the method given in techniques (pages 141 and 143). Fix a length of 9mm ribbon around the base of each cake with a little royal icing.

2 Roll out the coloured sugar pastes very finely to a thickness of 1–2mm. Press the outside of the heart cutter firmly to cut out the shape. Carefully lift the paste and depress the centre of the cutter (which is usually spring-loaded) to release the cut-out heart.

3 Randomly fix the hearts on to the cakes using sugar glue, allowing 7–8 per cake.

4 Colour some royal icing for the swirls. Fit the piping bag with the no. 1.5 nozzle and fill with the coloured royal icing. Pipe swirls on to a selection of the hearts, starting at the inside of the heart and working your way outwards. Allow to set for at least 6 hours before serving or packaging.

2

4

chocolate cups

These chocolate cups are perfect served as individual puddings for a dinner party or summer occasion. Each cup is surrounded with a chocolate collar and filled with fresh berries.

you will need

5cm round cakes

white chocolate plastique – allow 125g per cake plus 75g for the collars

icing sugar, for dusting

small rolling pin

pastry brush

brandy or cooled boiled water

cream grosgrain ribbon 15mm wide – allow 20cm per cake

small quantity royal icing

seasonal berries – raspberries, redcurrants, strawberries – allow 40g per cake

method

1 Cover each cake with an initial covering of white chocolate plastique, as shown in techniques page 149. Lightly dust a clean work surface with icing sugar. Roll out a 75g piece of white chocolate plastique to a rectangle measuring approximately 20 x 2.5cm. Trim the base edge with a sharp knife and feather the top edge using a small non-stick rolling pin.

2 Brush around the side of the cakes with brandy or cooled boiled water and wrap the collar around as shown. Use a sharp knife to trim the chocolate plastique so the two edges join.

3 Fix a length of cream grosgrain ribbon around the base of the cake with royal icing or melted chocolate and fill the cup with seasonal berries.

tip

Substitute dark chocolate for the white chocolate or have a combination of the two for a larger social gathering.

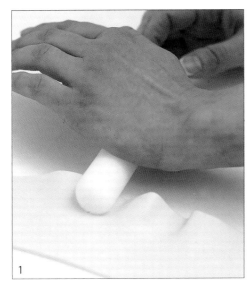

1

2

tricolour chocolate rose

Individually covered and decorated chocolate cakes make a fabulous gift presented together in a box. These cakes are perennially popular with clients of Little Venice Cake Company. They are often chosen as wedding cakes to be served for dessert: a perfectly presented chocolate cake for every guest.

you will need

5cm round cakes

white , milk or dark chocolate plastique for the roses – allow 5g each per rose and leaves

plastic sheeting

palette knife

white chocolate plastique for first coat – allow 60g per cake

white, milk or dark chocolate plastique for top coat – allow 75g per cake

piping bag

melted chocolate to fix ribbon and roses to the cake

grosgrain ribbon 15mm wide – allow 15cm per cake

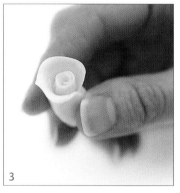

method

1 Make the roses. Warm a small amount of chocolate plastique between your palms and roll into a ball. Place between 2 sheets of plastic. Flatten quickly with the base of your palm, then, using your index finger, flatten two-thirds of the way round the ball, leaving a thicker base.

2 Remove the chocolate from the plastic sheeting and, holding the thicker base, gently roll the chocolate to form the centre of the rose.

3 Repeat step 1 to create 2 more petals. Wrap a petal around the rose centre, then fix the final petal so they overlap one another. Gently tease the petals into shape. Slice the base off the rose using a palette knife.

4 Allow for 3 roses and 3 leaves per cake. To make the leaves roll a small ball of dark chocolate plastique into a sausage approximately 2cm long and flatten into shape. Pinch the long sides together to form a leaf shape. Set aside to firm.

5 Cover the 5cm round cake with an initial coat of white chocolate plastique followed with a top coat as shown in the techniques, page 149. Fill a piping bag with a little melted chocolate and use to fix a length of grosgrain ribbon around the base of each cake and 3 roses and 3 leaves on top of each cake.

champagne primroses

This fresh design combines spring sugar primroses with delicately hand-piped champagne pearls. It would work particularly well with the light, fruity flavoured cakes – lime and coconut (page 80), banana butterscotch (page 85) or vanilla cake (page 83) with lemon curd buttercream (page 138) for all special occasions or summer picnics.

you will need

5cm round cakes

yellow petal paste – allow 20g per cake (3 primroses)

2.5cm primrose cutter

pale green dust

dipping alcohol

fine paintbrush

marzipan – allow 60g per cake

white sugar paste – allow 75g per cake

yellow ribbon 9mm wide – allow 15cm per cake

white royal icing

piping bag

no. 1.5 nozzle

method

1 To make the primroses, mould a marble-sized ball of yellow petal paste into a 'Mexican hat' – pinching and slightly hollowing the end as shown.

2 Place the 'hat' face down and fit the primrose cutter over the back and press down firmly and evenly on both sides of the cutter. Remove the excess paste. Pinch each petal carefully to thin the petals further.

3 Dissolve a little green dust in dipping alcohol and with a fine paintbrush paint the centre of the primrose as shown. Repeat for 3 primroses per cake and leave to dry and firm.

4 Cover each 5cm round cake with marzipan and sugar paste as shown in the techniques, pages 141 and 143. Fix a length of yellow ribbon around the base of each cake with a little royal icing.

5 Fill a piping bag with no. 1.5 nozzle and white royal icing. Pipe a cascade of pearls on to the cake at random intervals as shown. Fix the primroses on top with a dab of royal icing.

tip

For more variation make a variety of flowers and change the ribbons to complement.

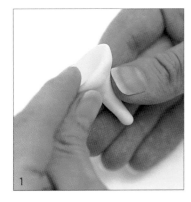

fondant red roses

These fondant cakes look very effective en masse. They have a sugar-moulded red rose in the centre of each cake framed by three hand piped green leaves. They work well with the lime and coconut cake (page 80, without the buttercream) or the vanilla cake (page 83) with added lemon or orange zest.

you will need

5cm round cakes

red sugar paste – allow 25g per rose

marzipan – allow 60g per cake

fondant icing – allow 75g per cake

6cm silver cup cake cases

ribbon or elastic bands to hold the cases in position

royal icing for the leaves

green edible food colour

piping bag

method

1 Use the red sugar paste to make the sugar moulded roses (see page 36) but make a centre and 4 more petals.

2 Cover the 5cm round cakes with marzipan and fondant icing as shown in the techniques, pages 141 and 144. Place each fondant covered cup cake in a silver case and hold in position with a tied length of plain ribbon or an elastic band until set.

3 Colour the royal icing with green food colouring. Fill a piping bag with the green royal icing and snip the end diagonally in both directions to form a 'V' as shown.

4 Holding the piping bag at the centre of the cup cake, pressure pipe 3 leaves tapering out towards the edge of the cake. Carefully position a sugar-moulded red rose into the centre and allow to set. Remove the ribbon or elastic band prior to serving.

apple blossom bears

Baby showers are increasing in popularity and are a lovely occasion to celebrate the impending arrival of a newborn baby. These gorgeous cakes would make the perfect accompaniment or could be posted out as a birth announcement cake. Alternatively, they could celebrate a baby's christening or first birthday. I think these cakes work especially well with our lime and coconut cake (page 80).

you will need

5cm square cakes

modelling paste – allow 30g per cake

teddy bear brown, light brown, black, blue and apple green edible food colours

modelling tools/cocktail stick

sugar glue

white royal icing – to fix the ribbon in position, pipe the eyes and to adhere the animals to the cakes

piping bags

2 no. 1.5 nozzles

very fine paintbrush

small rolling pin

white sugar paste – allow 90g per cake including the apple blossom flowers

small (3mm) and medium (5mm) flower plunger-cutters

marzipan – allow 70g per cake

white ribbon 15mm wide and apple green ribbon 6mm wide – allow 20cm each per cake

method

1 Make the teddy bears. Remove sufficient modelling paste to make the lighter brown muzzle and black nose and colour accordingly. Colour the remainder of the paste teddy-bear brown. Draw a 6cm square as a template and mould the paste into the body parts of the teddy bear as shown – ensuring the finished bear will fit inside the 6cm square template. Fix together with sugar glue, pipe the eyes with coloured royal icing – white, blue with a black pupil, and paint the mouth with black food colouring.

2 Roll a small amount of white sugar paste out thinly and plunge-cut the apple blossom flowers in two sizes. Allow to dry on a piece of tissue.

3 Cover the 5cm square cakes with marzipan and sugar paste as shown in techniques, pages 141 and 143. Fix a length of 15mm white ribbon overlaid with 6mm apple green ribbon around the base of each cake with a little royal icing. Using a piping bag filled with no. 1.5 nozzle and white royal icing, fix a garland of apple blossom flowers on to each cake as shown, concentrating on either the top corner or base corner for each cake. Pipe a white pearl into the centre of each flower. Fill another piping bag with pale apple green icing and a no. 1.5 nozzle and pipe tiny leaves between the flowers to finish.

4 Fix the teddy bears on to the top of some of the cakes with a dab of royal icing.

on the farm

These animal cakes are cute enough to bring out the child in all of us! I made these for an Easter charity morning at my son's school and also supplied them exclusively to Harvey Nichols for an Easter promotion. They make a lovely take-home gift for a child's birthday party – simply wrapped in a cotton napkin or individually boxed and ribboned. Choose a cake that is likely to appeal to children such as vanilla (page 83), chocolate almond (page 90) or lime and coconut (page 80).

you will need

5cm square cakes

marzipan – allow 70g per cake

white sugar paste – allow 85g per cake

party ribbon 9mm wide

royal icing – to fix the ribbon in position and the animals to the cakes

yellow, orange, brown, green, pink, black and white sugar paste for the animals

modelling tools/cocktail stick

sugar glue

method

1 Cover the 5cm square cakes with marzipan and sugar paste as shown in the techniques, pages 141 and 143. Fix a length of 9mm ribbon around the base of each cake with a little royal icing.

2 Make the animals – fixing everything in position with sugar glue. For the duck, mould an oval piece of yellow paste to form the head. Add the orange beak, eyes and yellow quiff at the top.

3 For the sheep, mould an oval piece of brown paste and use a knife to create a mouth. Add the eyes, 2 floppy ears and white balls of paste for the wool. Finish with green paste to resemble chewing grass.

4 For the pig start with a round piece of pink paste and flatten. Add the snout and use a marking tool to create the nostrils. Finish with the eyes and 2 ears.

5 Fix the animals on to the top of each cake with a dab of royal icing.

small
party cakes

small party cakes These are both stylish and elegant – showcasing a larger single tiered or multi-tiered cake creates drama, excitement and a real sense of occasion. They suit a more formal celebration as these cakes will create a natural photograph opportunity when gathering all the guests together for a champagne toast. I have presented a collection of my favourites in this chapter for weddings, anniversaries, birthdays, christenings as well as some fabulous Christmas cakes. These designs can be constructed from the cakes in the chapter *Delicious Treats*.

cherry blossom

There is a saying that a life spent searching for the perfect cherry blossom is a life well spent. Here is a perfect cherry blossom cake – combining soft brown and pink colours on two tiers. I have used the sticky date cake (page 86) as the base, but do please choose your favourite!

you will need

5cm and 7.5cm round cakes cut from 1 x 20cm square cake

150g marzipan

450g ivory sugar paste

12.5cm round cake board

greaseproof paper

scribe

white royal icing

chocolate brown, dark pink, and pale pink edible food colours

40cm pale pink ribbon 6mm wide, for the cakes

60cm chocolate brown ribbon 3mm wide, for the cakes and bow

3 piping bags

3 no. 1.5 nozzles

40cm dusky pink ribbon 15mm wide, for the board

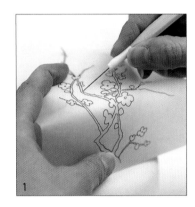

method

1 Cover the two round cakes with marzipan and sugar paste following the method given in techniques, pages 141 and 143, then stack centrally on a 12.5cm round cake board lined with ivory sugar paste.

2 Trace the cherry blossom design (page 153) on to a sheet of greaseproof or tracing paper and scribe on to the base and top tier of the cake. Colour one third of the royal icing with chocolate brown food colouring, one third with pink and one third a paler pink.

3 Fix a length of pink ribbon overlaid with brown ribbon around the base of each tier with a little royal icing. Tie a bow with a piece of brown ribbon and fix to the ribbon on the top tier, over the join, with a little royal icing. Fill 3 piping bags fitted with no. 1.5 nozzles with the different coloured royal icing. Beginning with the brown icing, pressure pipe the branches following the scribed design. With the pink icing, pipe pearls to make the cherry blossom, adding either a paler or darker pink centre for authenticity. Fix the 15mm ribbon round the cake board with a little royal icing.

little venice lace™

I designed this cake with London's Dorchester Hotel as the inspiration. The vintage hand-piped lace and pearl design is brushed with a pearlised lustre for a very special formal occasion such as an intimate wedding, wedding anniversary, engagement or civil partnership. The pattern can be traced and used on a larger tiered wedding cake for a more social gathering. This lace has become the iconic trademark of Little Venice Cake Company.

you will need

20cm square cake
600g marzipan
750g ivory sugar paste
greaseproof paper
scribe
piping bag
no. 2 nozzles
white royal icing
60cm ivory ribbon 9mm wide
topaz lustre
dipping alcohol
fine paintbrush
3 hand-moulded ivory roses and 8 rose leaves to decorate

method

1 Cut out a 15cm heart from the square cake. Following the techniques on pages 140 and 142, cover the heart with marzipan and sugar paste. Trace the lace design (page 154) on to a piece of tracing or greaseproof paper and position around the cake, ensuring the centre of one repeat is lined up with the point of the heart. Scribe the design on to the cake.

2 Fill a piping bag with a no. 2 nozzle and white royal icing. Fix a length of ribbon around the base of the cake with a little royal icing, then pressure pipe the design around the sides of the cake as shown. Allow to set for at least 4 hours.

3 Suspend a small amount (½ tsp) topaz lustre in dipping alcohol. Using a fine paintbrush, paint the lustre on to the entire design as shown. Dress the cake with lustred hand-moulded roses (page 36) and green rose leaves or a small corsage of fresh flowers tied with organza ribbon.

charleston pearls

This cake has been inspired by the 1920s Charleston pearls – endless strings of pearls worn in varying lengths and widths along with the traditional flapper dresses and feathers. This is a very bold design that transposes well on to a larger multi-tiered wedding cake or, as here, for an intimate wedding, dressed with fresh roses studded with crystals.

you will need

7.5cm and 12.5cm square cakes cut from 1 x 20cm square cake

850g marzipan

1kg white sugar paste

thin card

scribe

piping bag

no. 3 nozzle

white royal icing

1 metre white ribbon 15mm wide

paintbrush

clear edible gel

7 small headed white roses tied with white organza ribbon

12 clear crystals 12mm diameter

12 white wires gauge 28

method

1 Following the techniques on page 140 and 142, cover the 7.5cm and 12.5cm square cakes with marzipan and sugar paste and stack centrally. Trace the 3 templates from page 153 on to thin card and cut out. Scribe the different curves around the top edge of each tier, overlapping the designs as you work your way around.

2 Fill a piping bag with no. 3 nozzle and white royal icing. Fix a length of white ribbon around the base of each tier then begin piping the strands of pearls – making each slightly different – pressure piping different intensities as shown. Allow to set for at least 4 hours.

3 Using a paintbrush, brush each pearl with clear edible gel. To finish hand tie a small bouquet of fresh white roses with a length of white organza ribbon and bow. Thread crystals on to white wires gauge 28 and twist to secure. Trim the end of the wire to 2.5cm length and insert one crystal into the centre of each rose, and some between.

polka passion

Bright and vibrant, this pretty cake design was adopted by Harrods – with a showgirl leaping out of the top of a 3-tier version! I have worked with pink and green colours, but adapt these to complement your own theme. This design works equally well on a single tier or little individual cakes.

you will need

5cm and 7.5cm round cakes cut from 1 x 20cm square cake

150g marzipan

500g white sugar paste

12.5cm round cake board

leaf green, pale pink and darker pink edible food colours

white royal icing

icing sugar to dust

small rolling pin

polka dot plunger-cutter 1.5cm diameter

sugar glue

3 piping bags

3 no. 1.5 nozzles

40cm pretty ribbon 9mm wide, for the cakes

40cm fuchsia pink ribbon15mm wide, for the board

method

1 Following the techniques on page 141 and 143, cover the 5cm and 7.5cm round cakes with marzipan and sugar paste and stack centrally on a 12.5cm round cake board lined with white sugar paste.

2 Divide the remaining sugar paste equally into 3 and colour each with green, pale or darker pink. Divide the royal icing into 3 bowls and colour each with green, pale or darker pink to match the sugar paste. Lightly dust a work surface with icing sugar and roll out the 3 sugar paste colours. Plunge cut polka dots and use sugar glue to fix these into position on the cake randomly – ensuring the colours are well interspersed and there is space between the polka dots.

3 Fill 3 piping bags with no. 1.5 nozzles and the coloured royal icing in each. Fix a length of pretty ribbon around the base of each cake and pressure pipe pearls around the edge of each polka dot as shown – leaving sufficient space to pipe a second row. With a second colour, pipe elongated pearls between the first as shown. Finally, fix the pink ribbon around the cake board with a dab of royal icing.

metallic painted irises

Metallic lustres paint well on to smooth, dark chocolate. The effect
is quite Art Nouveau and here I have painted a collection of iris
flowers and butterflies using copper, dark bronze and gold lustres. This
is an expressive technique that allows you to be a free-flowing artist!

you will need

7.5cm and 10cm square cakes
cut from 1 x 20cm square cake

600g white chocolate plastique

850g dark chocolate plastique
covering

15cm square cake board

1 metre dark brown grosgrain
ribbon 15mm wide

greaseproof paper

scribe

bronze, copper and gold
metallic lustres

dipping alcohol

paintbrushes

method

1 Following the technique on page 149, cover the 7.5cm and 10cm square
cakes with an initial coat of white chocolate plastique with a top coat of dark
chocolate plastique covering, and stack offset on a 15cm square cake board
lined with dark chocolate plastique. Fix a length of grosgrain ribbon around
each cake and the base board.

2 Trace the flower and butterfly designs from page 156 on to greaseproof
or tracing paper.

3 Use a scribe to transfer the design on to the cake, decorating the sides
and the top of the cake.

4 Suspend the separate coloured metallic lustres in dipping alcohol and
paint the iris design and butterflies. Build up the layers to create depth
of colour.

tip

This technique would also work well on individual chocolate-covered cakes.

cannes-cannes

Inspired by the catwalk fashions of Chanel, this cake is the epitome of French elegance – Parisian chic and Cannes glamour! It works well in different colour combinations but I love the classic and sophisticated black and white look.

you will need

5cm and 10cm square cakes cut from 1 x 20cm square cake

450g marzipan

1 kg white sugar paste

10cm square cake board

250g petal paste

small rolling pin

brandy, for brushing

icing sugar, for dusting

pastry brush

cooled boiled water or sugar glue

1 metre black ribbon 9mm wide

royal icing to fix the ribbon

decorated cake stand (optional)

method

1 Following the technique on page 141 and 143 cover the 5cm and 10cm square cakes with marzipan and sugar paste and stack centrally on the cake board. Blend the remaining white sugar paste with the petal paste – this will allow the paste to set firmer holding its position. Lightly knead the paste then roll out to a collar length 50 x 9cm. Trim with a sharp knife then feather the upper edge of the collar with the small rolling pin.

2 Brush the sides of the base tier with brandy and fix the collar into position. Trim with a sharp knife to form a neat join at the back. Repeat with the top tier making a smaller collar, dimensions approximately 25 x 9cm, and applying as before.

3 Dust the work surface with a little icing sugar. Roll out small lengths of paste 15 x 3cm and feather the top edge. Gather the frills up as shown.

4 Brush the inside of the collar with cooled boiled water or sugar glue and fix the frills inside the collars. Repeat until the collars are completely filled with frills and allow to firm. Remove any excess icing sugar from the frills using a dry pastry brush.

5 Make 2 black ribbon bows. Fix a length of ribbon around each tier with royal icing at the back of the cake and finish with a ribbon bow on the front corner. Serve on a decorated cake stand, if you like.

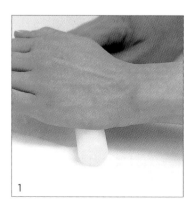

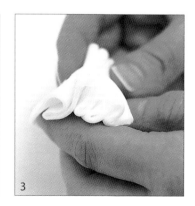
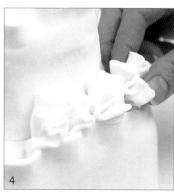

cascading roses and lilies

I have used alternate tiers of white and dark chocolate tumbling with a cascade of hand-moulded white and dark chocolate roses, lilies and leaves to create this contemporary chocolate design. Chocolate will complement any chocolate base cake, or opt for a light vanilla base with vanilla, chocolate or espresso buttercream.

you will need

5cm and 7.5cm round cakes cut from 1 x 20cm square cake

600g white chocolate plastique to cover and for the flowers

200g dark chocolate plastique for the flowers

ball modelling tool

small rolling pin

2cm rose veiner and cutter

500g dark chocolate plastique covering

12.5cm round cake board

20cm cream grosgrain ribbon 15mm wide

75cm dark brown grosgrain ribbon 15mm wide

2 piping bags

50g white chocolate, melted

50g dark chocolate, melted

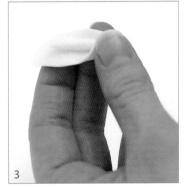

method

1 Make the flowers: roses, lilies and leaves. The exact number you will require will depend on the size of the flowers, the size of the tiers and how much of the cake you want to cover. For this cake I made 10 white chocolate roses, 5 lilies, 5 leaves; 6 dark chocolate roses, 3 lilies and 5 leaves. Follow the technique on page 36 for the roses, making a centre and 4 more petals.

2 For the arum lilies, roll a pea sized piece of paste into a sausage approximately 2.5cm long. Cut a triangular piece of paste and using a ball tool, thin out the edges.

3 Wrap this around the sausage to create the lily. Roll the remaining paste out and use a rose cutter to vein and cut out the leaves.

4 Following the techniques on page 149, cover the 5cm and 7.5cm round cakes with an initial coat of white chocolate plastique with a top coat of either white or dark chocolate plastique and stack centrally on a 12.5cm round cake board lined with dark chocolate plastique covering. Fix a length of grosgrain ribbon around each cake and the base board.

5 Fill 2 piping bags, one with melted white chocolate and one with melted dark chocolate. Starting with the dark chocolate flowers, fix these into position on the lower tier, working from the base board upwards. As the flowers join the upper tier switch to white chocolate flowers and finish with a topiary flourish on the top tier.

tip

It is always worth making more flowers than you might need to make sure you have enough to make a fabulous, full garland. Any spare flowers will keep in an airtight container for 6 months.

For larger or more tiers, wrap a 2.5cm thick sausage of paste from the top of the cake to the base board. This will act as a guide to follow when applying the flowers and also provide a good platform to adhere the flowers.

classic christmas rose

Christmas is a fabulous time of year for a celebration cake. I have included three Christmas cakes in this chapter – this design being the most traditional. You can modernise this cake by opting for a non-traditional flavour of cake inside such as the sticky date cake (page 86) or follow this design for your own favourite rich fruit cake recipe.

you will need

20cm round cake

small rolling pin

50g white petal paste

2.5cm rose cutter

ball modelling tool

sugar glue

white royal icing

yellow and red edible food colour

2 piping bag

2 no. 1.5 nozzles

fine paintbrush

leaf green colour dust

1kg marzipan

1.25kg white sugar paste

70cm each red ribbon 25mm wide, green ribbon 15mm wide, and white ribbon 6mm wide

75g holly green petal paste

2.5cm holly veiner and plunger-cutter

aluminium foil

2cm holly veiner and plunger-cutter

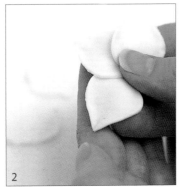

method

1 Make the 3 Christmas roses: roll out the white petal paste very thinly. Cut out 5 petals for each rose with the rose cutter. Use a ball modelling tool to thin the edges of the petal.

2 Lay 5 petals in a circle as shown, held in position with sugar glue. Pinch the tips of the rose petals. Colour 1 tbsp of the royal icing with yellow food colour. Fill a piping bag with a no. 1.5 nozzle and yellow royal icing. Pipe the centre of the rose as shown.

3 Brush the outer tips of the rose with green colour dust as shown and leave to dry. Repeat to make the other roses.

4 Following the techniques on page 140 and 142, cover the round cake with marzipan and sugar paste. Starting with the widest ribbon (red), fix around the cake, overlaid with the green and finally white ribbon. Fix with a dab of royal icing.

5 Roll out the green petal paste and vein and plunge-cut 6 x 2.5cm holly leaves for the top of the cake. Position these on a scrunched piece of aluminium foil to firm in a textured position. Meanwhile vein and plunge-cut 20–25 x 2cm green holly leaves. Position these around the side of the cake at a slight angle fixed into position with white royal icing. Colour 1 tbsp royal icing with red edible food colour. Fill a piping bag with a no. 1.5 nozzle and red royal icing. Pipe a single berry beneath each holly leaf around the cake. Fix the larger holly leaves and roses into position on the top of the cake with royal icing, and finish by piping the red berries on the top beside the holly.

tip

Petal paste dries out very quickly so only work on one rose at a time. Once the rose has been made it will set firm within a couple of hours. Because it has a higher quantity of gum tragacanth it can be rolled much thinner than sugar paste, creating more delicate flowers.

sugar candy

Our candy stripe design has become synonymous with Little Venice Cake Company. Here I have used various widths of coloured sugar paste around two tiers of cake and added some hand-iced sugar butterflies – made a couple of days beforehand – for real party pizzazz.

you will need

5cm and 10cm round cakes cut from 1 x 20cm square cake

500g marzipan

1.25kg white sugar paste (colour 250g fuchsia pink for the board)

15cm round cake board

fuchsia pink, buttercup yellow, tangerine orange and leaf green edible food colours

scribe

small rolling pin

icing sugar, for dusting

sugar glue

50cm fuchsia pink ribbon 15mm wide, for the board

for the butterflies

tracing and waxed paper

masking tape

edible food colours

no. 1.5 and no. 3 nozzles

piping bags

white royal icing

fine paintbrush

cocktail stick

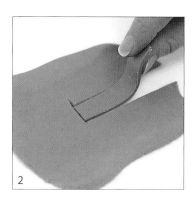 

method

1 Following the techniques on pages 141 and 143, cover the 5cm and 10cm round cakes with marzipan and white sugar paste and stack centrally on a 15cm round cake board lined with fuchsia pink sugar paste.

2 Divide the remaining sugar paste equally into 4, and colour each with fuchsia pink, buttercup yellow, tangerine orange or leaf green to the desired intensity. Scribe around the top of each cake as a guideline. Roll out the paste very finely on a work surface lightly dusted with icing sugar. Cut the paste into strips of varying widths. Don't prepare too many in advance as the paste will dry out. Cover any prepared strips with cling film.

3 Use the sugar glue to fix the strips into position around the sides of each tier of the cake as shown, making sure the strip butts up to the preceding strip. Trim the end of each strip to your scribed guideline with a sharp knife.

4 Finish with 5 hand made iced butterflies made using the run-out method as shown in the techniques on page 145. Fix the pink ribbon round the board with a small quantity of royal icing.

sleeping polar bear

This polar bear reminds me of my son George – he looks so angelic when fast asleep. I have domed the top of the cake and laid a sheet of white sugar paste over a blue iced cake to resemble an iceberg. With the holly and berries on top of his head he looks as though he has filled his tummy with a hearty Christmas lunch – just as it should be!

you will need

15cm round cake plus extra cake to add a dome on the top (all cut from 1 x 20cm cake)

buttercream or apricot jam

1kg blue sugar paste

750g marzipan

23cm round cake board

1.25 metre blue ribbon 15mm wide

small rolling pin

500g white sugar paste

sharp knife

brandy or cooled boiled water

pastry brush

modelling tools

fine paintbrush

black, holly green and red edible food colours

holly leaf veiner and plunger-cutter

craft knife

sugar glue

white royal icing

piping bag

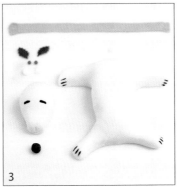

method

1 Cut out a 15cm round cake and pack extra cake on the top to create a dome shape. Use buttercream or apricot jam to hold in place. Reserve a small quantity of blue sugar paste for the scarf. Following the techniques on pages 140 and 142, cover the cake with marzipan and blue sugar paste and place on a 23cm round cake board lined with blue sugar paste. Fix a length of ribbon around the base of the cake and the cake board.

2 Roll out 200g white sugar paste to approximately 15cm round. Cut the outline with a sharp knife. Brush the top of the cake with brandy or cooled boiled water and lay the white sugar paste over the top of the cake.

3 Make the polar bear: mould white sugar paste into a body with 4 legs; a head, small tail and 2 ears. Paint the toes with black edible colour and a fine paintbrush. Colour a little paste black and make a nose and 2 eyes.

4 Colour some paste green and cut out the 2 holly leaves; colour a little paste red and make berries. Using the reserved blue paste, roll out to create a scarf. Cut the ends with a fine craft knife to make a fringe. While the paste is still malleable construct the polar bear directly on to the cake so it moulds to the shape – use sugar glue to hold the pieces together. Wrap the scarf around the head before fixing into position. Place a small amount of white royal icing in a piping bag, and use to fix the holly and berries into position.

bunny building block

This cake is inspired by a child's building block. I have made the cake very deep to create a cube – stack three layers of cake with two layers of buttercream before covering with marzipan and sugar paste. You can change the colour of the icing for a special little girl or boy or make three cakes of different sizes and have a trio of building blocks.

you will need

10cm cube cake (cut out from a 20cm square cake)

600g marzipan

1kg yellow sugar paste

15cm square cake board

50cm white ribbon 9mm wide, for the cake

65cm white ribbon 15mm wide, for the board

white royal icing

250g white sugar paste for the bunny

modelling tools

black and pink edible food colours for the nose and eyes

sugar glue

small rolling pin

200g white sugar paste for the panels

tracing or greaseproof paper

50g yellow petal paste for the letters

scalpel

method

1 Following the techniques on pages 140 and 142, cover the cube cake with marzipan and yellow sugar paste and place on a 15cm square cake board lined with yellow sugar paste. Fix a length of ribbon around the base of the cake and the cake board with a little royal icing.

2 Make the bunny: mould the white sugar paste into a body, head, ears, tail, jowls, eyes and teeth. Colour a small amount into black for the eyes and pink for the nose. While the paste is still malleable, construct the bunny directly on to the cake so it moulds to the shape – use sugar glue to hold the components together.

3 Roll out the white sugar paste for the panels and cut into 5 panels each 6cm square. Fix these into position on the sides and top of the cake with sugar glue. Trace and cut out the alphabet letters from page 152. Roll out the yellow petal paste very thinly and use a scalpel to cut out each letter.

4 Position one letter on each of the 4 sides of the cake (you don't need one for the top) and fix into position with sugar glue.

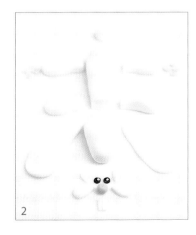

elephant polka dot

I love the way this elephant is clambering up and over the edge of the cake. This charming design is perfect for a child's birthday party. You could make smaller elephant heads and use them on the top of individual cakes, or a family of these whole elephants climbing over a tiered cake for a larger party.

you will need

20cm oval cake (bake in an oval tin or cut out from a square cake)

800g marzipan

1.3kg white sugar paste

27.5cm oval cake board

1.5 metre blue ribbon 15mm wide

white royal icing

250g grey sugar paste

modelling tools

sugar glue

shades of blue and black edible food colours

piping bags

no. 1.5 nozzles

small rolling pin

1.5cm, 2cm and 3cm circle cutters

method

1 Following the techniques on pages 140 and 142, cover the oval cake with marzipan and sugar paste and place on an 27.5cm oval cake board lined with white sugar paste. Fix a length of ribbon around the base of the cake and the cake board with a little royal icing.

2 Make the elephant: mould the grey sugar paste into a body, head with trunk, 4 legs, 2 ears, eyelids and trunk end. Mould white feet pads and toes, tusks and white eyes. While the paste is still malleable, construct the elephant directly on to the cake so it moulds to the shape; use sugar glue to hold the pieces together. Colour a small amount of royal icing black, and pipe the eye pupils.

3 Divide the remainder of the sugar paste into 3 and colour one third pale blue, one third dark blue and keep one third white. Roll out the coloured sugar paste very finely to a thickness of 1–2mm. Press the outside of the cutter firmly to cut out the shapes. Carefully lift the paste and depress the centre, which is usually spring loaded to release the cut out shape. Cut out circles of all 3 colours and fix on to the cake with sugar glue.

4 Fill piping bags with no. 1.5 nozzles and white, pale blue or navy royal icing. Pipe a swirl on some of the circles working from the centre outwards.

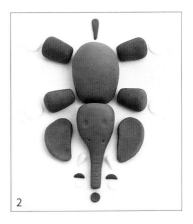

santa star

I was inspired by a Christmas star decoration that Santa left for each of my sons in their stockings last year! This is a simple design that can be made with the children for a very effective Christmas cake; all the components are cut out using the templates and built up in three layers. Make the pieces well in advance and decorate a cake on the run up to Christmas. Make a number of these for great gifts!

you will need

15cm round cake

600g marzipan

1.5kg white sugar paste to cover the cake and board

23cm round cake board

50cm red ribbon 15mm wide

1 metre red ribbon 35mm wide

350g white sugar paste

blue, black, green, pink, yellow and red edible food colours

small rolling pin

tracing or greaseproof paper

craft knife

sugar glue

modelling tools

pink dust

fine paintbrush

piping bag

black royal icing for the eyes

method

1 Following the techniques on pages 140 and 142, cover the cake with marzipan and white sugar paste and place on a 23cm round cake board lined with white sugar paste. Fix a length of ribbon around the cake board, tie the wider ribbon around the base of the cake and finish with a double bow.

2 Colour the paste for the Santa star as follows: a walnut-sized piece pale blue, a walnut-sized piece black, a walnut-sized piece green, a hazelnut-sized piece pale pink, a pea-sized piece yellow; a walnut-sized piece white and the remainder red.

3 To make the Santa star, start with the base red star which will form the body. Roll out the paste to a thickness of 4mm and use the template on page 157 to trace and cut out a star with the craft knife. You can either fix this directly on to the top of the iced cake or place on a board dusted heavily with icing sugar and allow to dry before icing all together and fixing in to position later. Roll out and build up the second layer, using the templates to trace and cut out the gloves, boots, belt, tree, hat trim, face and beard in the colours shown. Fix into position with sugar glue. Finish with the top layer – moustache, nose and bobble for the hat. Dust Santa's cheeks with pink dust and a paintbrush until they are big and rosy! Pipe 2 black eyes using royal icing.

delicious treats

delicious treats In this chapter I give a collection of cake recipes that are delicious to eat – just as they are – for a weekend treat. Alternatively they can be covered with marzipan and icing or chocolate and hand decorated. Whether your preference is for a rich, dark chocolate velvet cake or a lighter summer lime and coconut flavour, there is a recipe for all occasions. Throughout the book I have given my own personal cake preferences for each design – but this is by no means exhaustive and you can change the flavours to suit your own party occasion.

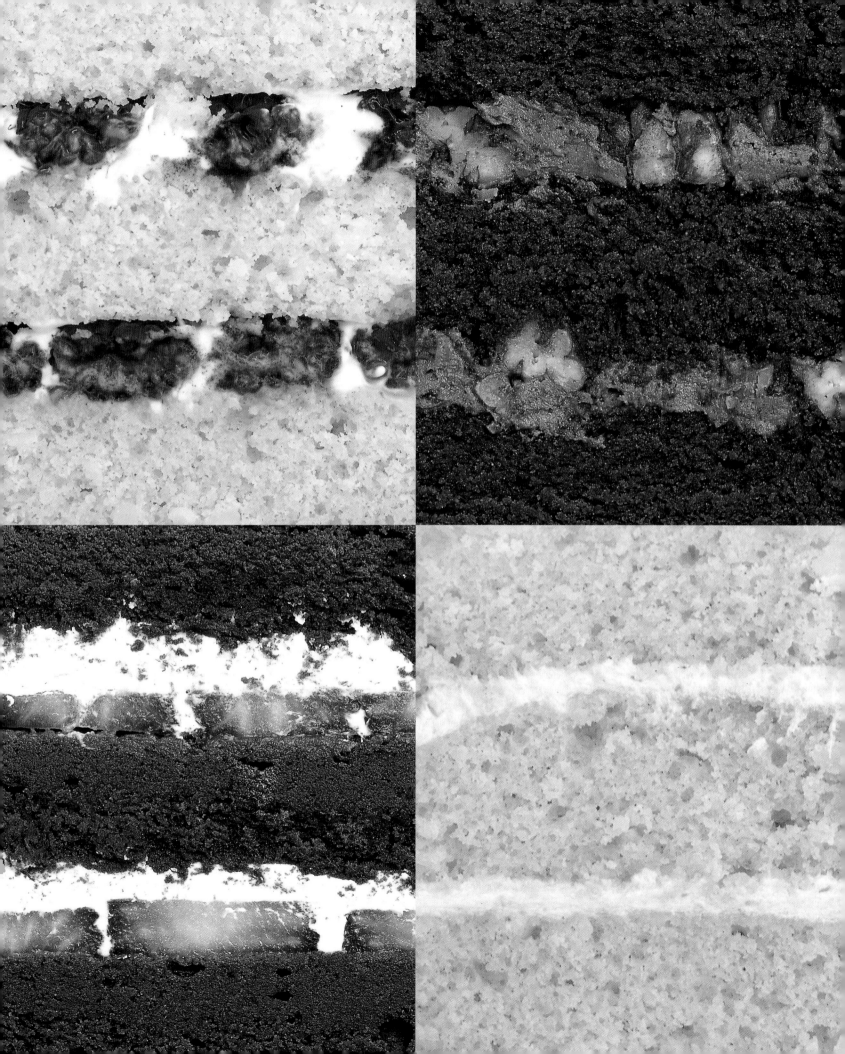

lime and coconut

This is a beautiful fresh cake combining the zest of fresh limes with creamed coconut. This cake is delicious to enjoy as it is or use it as a base either for small or tiered party cakes or individual cakes covered with icing and decoration as featured in earlier chapters.

for the cake

200g unsalted butter, softened
200g golden caster sugar
200g self raising flour
4 free range eggs, lightly beaten
2 tbsp milk
200g block of creamed coconut

for the buttercream

zest and juice of 2 limes
100g unsalted butter, softened
140g icing sugar
50g toasted desiccated coconut to finish (or flakes)

method

1 Preheat oven to 190°C (fan oven 170°C). Grease two 20cm loose-bottomed sandwich tins and line the base with non-stick baking parchment. Grate the 200g block of creamed coconut and keep half of it to one side.

2 Measure all the cake ingredients including half the creamed coconut into a large bowl and whisk together until you have a smooth batter.

3 Divide the mixture into the two sandwich tins, smooth the surface and bake in the oven for 20–25 minutes until risen, light golden and the cake springs back when pressed.

4 For the buttercream, mix together the reserved creamed coconut, zest and juice of 2 limes. Microwave or place over a pan of simmering water until the coconut melts. Allow to cool. Beat the butter until smooth and creamy, add the icing sugar and whisk slowly at first then at full speed until light and fluffy. Stir in the cooled coconut-lime mixture and whisk until light and marshmallowy.

5 Sandwich the cakes with half of the buttercream and use the remainder on the top and sides of the cake. Sprinkle with the toasted coconut.

storage

Store in an airtight container and eat within 2 days. Not suitable for freezing.

tip

For individual cakes, bake 2 square halves then use each separately; split horizontally and fill with a thin layer of the buttercream.

vanilla with fresh raspberries

This vanilla cake is delicious served with fresh raspberries and mascarpone for a special treat. Other fresh berries can be substituted and the cake itself can be used for any of the covered and decorated designs featured in earlier chapters – especially the fondant cakes – if the filling is replaced with the Madagascan vanilla buttercream.

for the cake

225g unsalted butter, softened

225g golden caster sugar

1 tbsp vanilla paste

4 large free range eggs, lightly beaten

225g self raising flour

3 tbsp milk

for the filling and decoration

40g icing sugar

8 tbsp mascarpone

200g fresh raspberries

method

1 Preheat oven to 170°C (fan oven 150°C). Grease two 20cm loose-bottomed sandwich tins and line the base with non-stick baking parchment. Dust the sides with a little flour.

2 Using a hand mixer, cream together the butter and sugar until light and fluffy. Stir in the vanilla paste. Add the eggs a little at a time until well incorporated. If the mixture starts to separate and curdle, stir in 1tbsp flour.

3 Fold in the remaining flour and stir in enough milk for a dropping consistency: the mixture should drop from the spoon by the count of three.

4 Spoon the mixture into the prepared tins. Level the top and bake in the oven for 25–30 minutes until well risen and a knife inserted in the centre comes out clean. Allow to cool slightly before turning out on to a wire rack.

5 Fold the icing sugar into the mascarpone then spread half over the bottom cake. Scatter half the raspberries on top. Place the other cake on top and repeat the mascarpone and raspberry layers. The cake can be kept up to 4 days ahead and stored in an airtight container. Refrigerate once filled with mascarpone and eat within 24 hours. Freezes for one month.

alternative filling

75g unsalted butter, softened

150g icing sugar

2 tsp Madagascan vanilla extract

Madagascan vanilla buttercream

Cream the butter with an electric whisk for 2 minutes until light and fluffy. Add the icing sugar and whisk slowly until incorporated then on high speed until very light and fluffy. Whisk in the vanilla extract. Keeps for one week in the fridge; allow to come up to room temperature before using and whisk again.

banana butterscotch

The combination of smooth butterscotch and baked bananas makes this the perfect cake for afternoon tea on cold days. The butterscotch is poured into the cake as soon as it is baked, which keeps the cake lovely and moist, making it an ideal choice for further covering with marzipan, icing and hand decoration.

for the cake

150g unsalted butter

300g self raising flour

150g golden caster sugar

50g sultanas

50g chopped walnuts

450g bananas, mashed

2 free range eggs

2 tsp vanilla extract

for the butterscotch

50g soft brown sugar

35g unsalted butter

2 tbsp double cream

method

1 Preheat oven to 180°C (fan oven 160°C). Grease a 20cm round cake tin and line the base with non-stick baking parchment.

2 Rub the butter into the flour until the mixture resembles fine breadcrumbs. Add the sugar, sultanas and chopped walnuts. Whisk the bananas and eggs together until very thick and creamy, then fold in the dry ingredients and the vanilla extract.

3 Transfer to the prepared tin and bake in the oven for 1 hour 15 minutes until risen and firm to the touch.

4 About 10 minutes before the cake is due to come out of the oven, measure the butterscotch ingredients into a small saucepan and heat gently until the sugar has completely dissolved and is bubbling. As soon as the cake comes out of the oven, pierce it all over with a skewer and pour the bubbling butterscotch over the top. Leave to cool in the tin.

tip

For individual cakes, the cake will need to be split horizontally before cutting out the rounds or squares.

sticky date

When we baked the collection of cakes in this chapter, this one was a clear favourite amongst the editorial team. It is moist, sticky and full of flavour. Because it requires no filling, this cake is an ideal choice for the base of the covered and decorated cakes in earlier chapters. It will stack well and keeps for a week once covered.

ingredients

200g dates, stoned

200g unsalted butter, cut into pieces

300g dark muscovado sugar

2 free range eggs

50g chopped stem ginger

grated zest of 1 lemon

1 tsp vanilla extract

250g bramley cooking apple, grated

200g self raising flour

icing sugar, for dusting

method

1 Preheat oven to 160°C (fan oven 140°C). Grease an 20cm round Kugelhopf cake tin.

2 Place the dates in a bowl and cover with boiling water. Melt the butter and sugar together in a saucepan and allow to cool slightly.

3 Beat the eggs, ginger, lemon zest and vanilla extract into the butter and sugar. Drain the dates and chop finely. Add to the saucepan and mix well.

4 Stir in the apple and flour, then spoon into the tin and bake in the oven for about 1 hour 15 minutes until well risen. When done, a skewer inserted should come out clean with a few crumbs. Leave to cool in the tin.

5 Dust the top with icing sugar to serve.

storage
Cake keeps a week stored in an airtight container or for 1 month frozen.

cherry and almond

This is a lovely moist cake as it combines fresh pitted cherries with a delicious crumble topping. Use the freshest, ripest cherries you can find. The finished cake is quite shallow which makes it the perfect depth for stamping out individual canapé sized rounds to serve at a summer buffet party. It wouldn't require much accompaniment – maybe a nice spoonful of crème fraîche. Because the cake contains fresh fruit it is not suitable for covering with marzipan and icing and it needs to be eaten fresh or stored refrigerated.

for the cake

140g self raising flour

50g golden caster sugar

1 large egg

4 tbsp organic milk

85g unsalted butter, melted

1 tsp almond extract

350g juicy ripe cherries

icing sugar, for dusting

for the crumble topping

25g butter at room temperature

25g ground almonds

25g golden caster sugar

$\frac{1}{2}$ tsp almond extract

method

1 Preheat oven to 180°C (fan oven 160°C). Grease and line the base of a shallow 20cm cake tin. Measure the flour and caster sugar into a bowl, stir together. Make a well in the centre and add the egg, milk, melted butter and almond extract. Beat with an electric whisk to make a smooth mixture. Spoon into the tin and spread evenly.

2 Remove the stalks and stones from the cherries, cut in half and scatter over the cake mixture – gently press them in.

3 Make the topping by measuring all the ingredients into a clean bowl. Rub the butter in until the mixture resembles fine breadcrumbs and then gently clumps together. Scatter this over the cherries.

4 Bake for 30–35 minutes until a skewer inserted in the centre of the cake comes out clean.

5 Allow the cake to cool before removing from the tin and allow to cool completely on a wire rack.

6 Dredge with icing sugar to serve.

tip

Try substituting the fresh cherries with other ripe fruit in season – plums and apricots work particularly well – chop the stoned flesh into quarters before adding to the recipe.

chocolate and almond

This is a rich, indulgent chocolate cake baked without flour. The ground almonds provide a nutty taste and texture and it holds together well and cuts beautifully. It is naturally shallow which makes it a perfect cake for cutting out individual shapes to be used in the designs in earlier chapters of this book.

ingredients

100g unsalted butter, diced plus extra for greasing

flour for dusting

140g chocolate (70% cocoa solids), broken into pieces

6 large free range eggs, separated

140g ground almonds

1 tsp almond extract

85g golden caster sugar

cocoa powder and crème fraîche, to serve

method

1 Preheat oven to 170°C (fan oven 150°C). Grease a 23cm loose-bottomed tin and line the base with non-stick baking parchment. Dust the sides with a little flour.

2 Melt the unsalted butter and chocolate together in a bowl over a pan of simmering water – stir occasionally until smooth. Leave for 5 minutes to cool slightly.

3 Stir in the egg yolks, ground almonds and almond extract.

4 Whisk the egg whites in a separate clean bowl until soft peaks form. Continue whisking adding the sugar a spoonful at a time. Whisk well between each addition until all is incorporated and stiff peaks form.

5 Stir 2 tbsp egg white into the chocolate mixture then gently fold in the remainder.

6 Spoon the mixture into the prepared tin and bake for 30–35 minutes until well risen and just firm to the touch. Dust with cocoa powder and serve with a spoonful of crème fraîche.

storage

Can be kept up to 4 days ahead and stored in an airtight container. Freezes for one month.

espresso bites

These bites are ideal for entertaining guests with morning coffee or to serve as after-dinner treats. I have used the chocolate almond cake (page 90) as the base, as this cake is naturally shallow and very 'chocolatey'. The espresso buttercream is flavoured with real fresh roasted espresso coffee and decorated with chocolate-covered espresso beans.

yields 25 bites

you will need

single layer 20cm square cake, cut into 5cm x 4cm slices

piping bag

large star nozzle

cocoa

50 chocolate-covered espresso beans

espresso buttercream

espresso, made with 100g fresh espresso coffee and 200ml fresh boiled water

250g unsalted butter, softened

500g icing sugar, sieved

method

1 Cut the square chocolate cake into 25 slices, each measuring 5cm x 4cm.

2 Make the espresso buttercream. Make the coffee in a cafetière. Pour freshly boiled water on to the fresh ground coffee and allow to steep for 5 minutes. Strain the espresso and leave to cool slightly. Beat the unsalted butter until light and creamy. Add the icing sugar and beat initially on slow then on high speed for 3 minutes. Stir in the espresso until you have the desired intensity of flavour.

3 Fill a piping bag with a large star nozzle and the espresso buttercream. Pipe a swirl design of buttercream on to the top of each bite as shown. Sieve a small amount of cocoa on to the top of each bite then finish with 2 chocolate covered espresso beans on each cake.

3

tip

This technique would work equally well with the lime and coconut cake with the lime and coconut buttercream or the vanilla cake with vanilla buttercream. Serve a selection together for a large social gathering or party.

chocca mocca pecan

This cake has the perfect blend of smooth chocolate, fresh espresso and toasted pecans. Delicious as a weekend cake to serve for family and friends, it can also be used as a base for any of the covered and decorated cakes throughout this book – especially the larger decorated celebration cakes and tiered options, whether covered with icing, fondant or chocolate.

for the cake

150g dark chocolate

4 tbsp strong espresso

175g unsalted butter, softened

175g golden caster sugar

5 large free range eggs, lightly beaten

100g finely chopped pecans

100g self raising flour

1 tsp baking powder

for the filling and decoration

100g dark chocolate

50g unsalted butter

3 tsp espresso coffee (use 3 rounded tablespoons of fresh coffee with 200ml of freshly boiled water, then plunge in a cafetière)

4 tbsp double cream

50g icing sugar

50g toasted pecans, roughly chopped

method

1 Preheat oven to 180°C (fan oven 160°C). Grease a 20cm loose-bottomed tin and line the base with non-stick baking parchment.

2 Melt the chocolate and espresso together over a pan of simmering water and stir until smooth. Allow to cool slightly.

3 Using a hand mixer cream together the butter and sugar until light and fluffy. Beat in the eggs a little at a time until well incorporated. Don't worry if the mixture starts to separate and curdle, it won't affect the finished cake.

4 Pour in the chocolate mixture and add the pecans; stir until combined.

5 Sieve the flour and baking powder together in a separate bowl then gently fold into the cake mixture.

6 Spoon the mixture into the prepared tin and bake in the oven for 45–55 minutes until firm to the touch. Allow to cool slightly before turning out on to a wire rack to cool completely. Place the pecans for toasting on a baking tray and place in the oven for the final 10 minutes baking time. Remove and allow to cool before roughly chopping.

to make the filling

1 Put the chocolate, butter, espresso and cream in a small pan and heat gently until dissolved and smooth. Remove from the heat and stir in the icing sugar. Leave to cool then refrigerate for 1–2 hours until thick enough to spread.

2 Slice the cake horizontally and spread with half the filling. Scatter with half the toasted pecans. Cover with the other half of the cake, spread the remaining filling on the top and finish with the remaining toasted pecans.

fluffy desserts

fluffy desserts

I have had so much fun presenting – and tasting – this range of fabulous desserts and puddings. From creamy cheesecakes, to rich roulades and mouthwatering meringues, these desserts make a fabulous addition to lunch or dinner parties and afternoon teas. Visually stunning and delicious to eat, they are guaranteed to impress and take only a fraction of the time of fully decorated cakes.

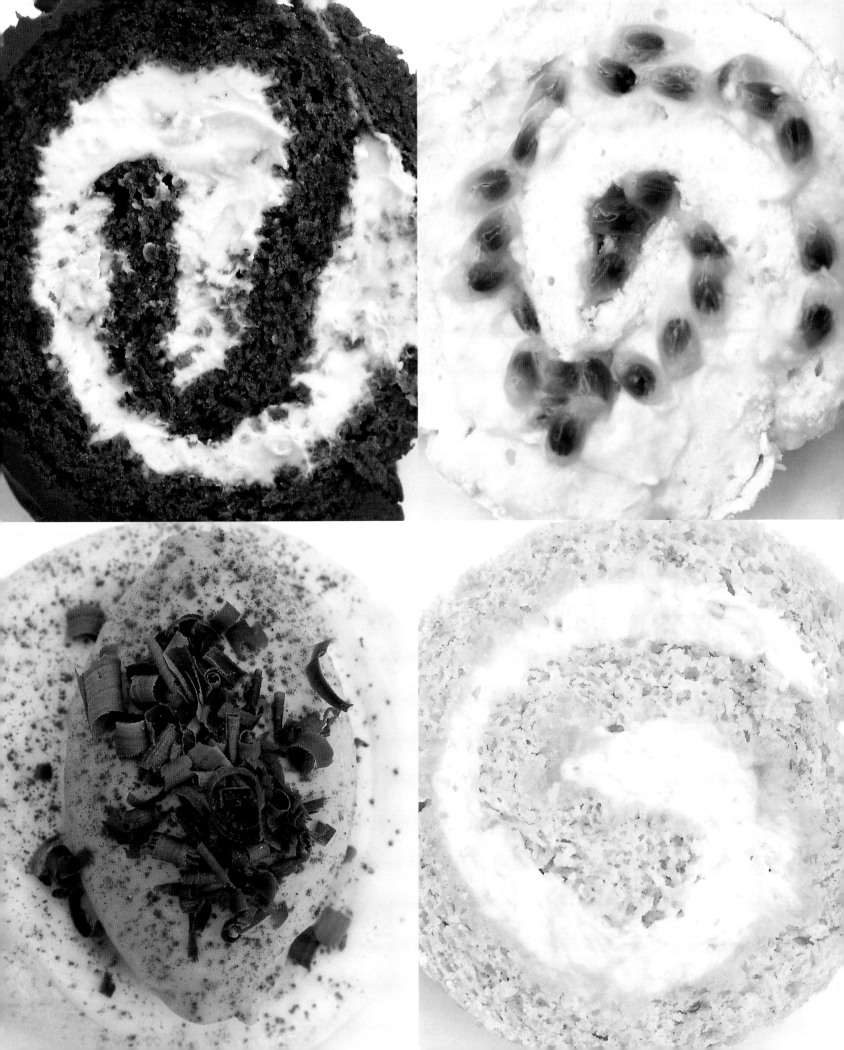

mango and ginger cheesecake

This recipe is one of my personal favourites and never fails to impress. It is simple to make as it needs no baking or setting agent: it relies on the weight of the cheese and cream to set the cheesecake. The combination of stem ginger and fresh mango purée is absolutely delicious.

8–10 servings

fills 8 x 7.5cm fluted tart cases or 1 x 20cm round

ingredients

100g unsalted butter

200g digestive biscuits, crushed

300g fresh cream cheese

150g golden caster sugar

2 drops vanilla extract

400ml whipping cream

200g fresh mango

2 pieces stem ginger, chopped

2 tbsp stem ginger syrup

method

1 Melt the butter in a saucepan and stir in the crushed biscuits. Press into the base of a loose-bottomed 20cm cake tin and refrigerate for 1 hour or until set.

2 Beat the cream cheese, caster sugar and vanilla until light and fluffy. Add the cream and beat until stiff (but do not overbeat or the mixture will separate).

3 Blitz the fresh mango until it forms a thick purée. Stir 4 tbsp of the mango and the chopped stem ginger into the cheesecake mix.

4 Spread the cheesecake mix on top of the biscuit base and refrigerate overnight.

to serve

Stir the stem ginger syrup into the remaining mango purée and serve on the side.

chocolate cheesecake

A real adult's cheesecake and definitely one for chocoholics – for a more family-friendly version omit the Kahlua. This cheesecake can be made a day in advance and the topping added just prior to serving.

for the base

50g unsalted butter

200g plain chocolate digestive biscuits, crushed

50g amaretti biscuits, crushed

for the filling

225g dark chocolate (minimum 55% cocoa solids), broken

400g full fat cream cheese, at room temperature

100g golden caster sugar

4 medium eggs

284ml double cream

5 tbsp Kahlua (optional)

for the topping

200ml crème fraîche

2 tbsp Kahlua (optional)

cocoa powder for dusting

50g amaretti biscuits, crushed

method

1 Melt the butter in a saucepan and stir in the crushed biscuits. Press into the base of a non-stick 20cm loose-bottomed cake tin and refrigerate for 1 hour or until set.

2 Make the filling: melt the chocolate in a bowl over a pan of gently simmering water and allow to cool. Heat the oven to 160°C (fan oven 140°C).

3 Beat the cream cheese and caster sugar until light and fluffy. Add the eggs one at a time but don't overbeat. Blend in the melted chocolate, the cream and Kahlua, if using, slowly until combined then pour the cheesecake mix on top of the biscuit base. Bake in the oven for 1 hour until set. Run a knife around the inside of the tin to loosen the cheesecake then refrigerate overnight.

to serve

1 To serve, combine the crème fraiche with the Kahlua, if using, and spread over the top of the cheesecake.

2 Mix the cocoa powder with the crushed amaretti biscuits and sprinkle over the top.

blackcurrant cheesecake

This cheesecake has a traditional New York-style soured cream cheesecake base which is deliciously creamy. I have added the sharpness of a blackcurrant compôte as I grow the fruit in my garden and look forward to the juiciest crop for making this recipe every year. It makes a fabulous dinner party pudding and can be made a day in advance.

for the base

85g unsalted butter plus extra for brushing the tin

140g digestive biscuits, crushed

for the cheesecake filling

900g full fat cream cheese

250g golden caster sugar

3 tbsp plain flour

1½ tsp vanilla extract

grated zest of 1 lemon

1½ tsp lemon juice

3 large eggs plus 1 yolk

284ml carton soured cream

for the topping

142ml carton soured cream

1 tbsp golden caster sugar

2 tsp lemon juice

600g blackcurrants

85g sugar

method

1 Heat the oven to 180°C (fan oven 160°C). Line the base of a 23cm springform cake tin with non-stick paper. Melt the butter in a saucepan and stir in the crushed biscuits. Press into the base of the tin and bake for 10 minutes – allow to cool on a wire rack while preparing the filling.

2 Turn the oven up to 240°C (fan oven 200°C). In a large bowl, beat the cream cheese by itself until creamy, then slowly add the sugar and flour. Add the vanilla, lemon zest and juice and whisk for 2 minutes. Add the eggs and yolk one at a time. Stir the carton of soured cream then add 200ml to the cheesecake mixture (reserving the rest) and whisk gently until smooth, light and airy.

3 Place the tin on a baking sheet. Brush the sides of the tin with melted butter, then carefully pour in the cheesecake batter. Bake for 10 minutes then reduce the heat to 110°C (fan oven 90°C) and bake for a further 25 minutes. Turn off the oven and open the door. Allow the cheesecake to cool for 2 hours. The cheesecake may crack slightly on the top as it cools.

4 Make the topping: combine the reserved soured cream with the 142ml carton, the sugar and lemon juice. Spread over the top of the cheesecake right to the edges. Cover loosely with foil and refrigerate for at least 8 hours or overnight.

5 Wash, top and tail the blackcurrants and place in a saucepan with the sugar and a splash of water. Bring to the boil, then reduce the heat and simmer gently until the fruit has all broken up, 15–20 minutes. Remove from the heat and refrigerate overnight.

to serve

Run a round-bladed knife around the sides of the tin to loosen any stuck edges. Transfer the cheesecake on to a plate, and spoon the blackcurrants on the top.

chocolate strawberry torte

Chocolate and strawberries have such an affinity. This is an impressive recipe to serve for pudding; it encompasses layers of chocolate truffle torte sandwiched with fresh cream and succulent strawberries. The cake is smothered with a layer of chocolate buttercream before being covered with a deliciously wicked, thick chocolate glaze.

serves 12

for the cake

200g plain chocolate (70% cocoa solids), broken into pieces

250g unsalted butter

350g light brown sugar

5 medium eggs, beaten

1½ tsp vanilla extract

135g plain flour, sieved

for the filling

200g fresh strawberries

284ml fresh double cream

to finish

1 quantity chocolate ganache buttercream (see page 139)

500g dark chocolate (70% cocoa solids), broken into pieces

250g unsalted butter, cut into small pieces

125ml double cream

100g dark chocolate shards

method

1 Preheat the oven to 160°C (fan oven 140°C). Melt the chocolate carefully in a microwave or bowl over simmering water, then allow to cool. Have all the ingredients at room temperature. Grease and line a 20cm tin. Beat together the butter and sugar until and light and fluffy. Add the beaten egg a little at a time until all is incorporated.

2 Pour the cooled melted chocolate slowly into the creamed mixture, beating all the time. Stir in the vanilla extract, then fold in the sieved flour.

3 Pour the mixture in the tin and bake for 1 hour until risen and lightly set. The cake should still wobble when shaken lightly. Remove the cake from the oven and allow to cool before turning on to a wire rack. The crust should crack and sink back on to the cake.

4 To fill, carefully split the cake in half horizontally. Slice the fresh strawberries over the base. Lightly whip the cream and spread on top of the strawberries. Place the other cake layer on top. Stand the cake on a wire rack over a piece of non-stick baking paper.

5 Make the chocolate ganache buttercream (see page 139). Using a palette knife, spread the buttercream over the top and sides of the cake filling all the gaps and leaving clean sharp edges and sides. Refrigerate for 30 minutes to firm before glazing.

6 Make the chocolate glaze. Place the chocolate and butter in a bowl. In a pan, bring the cream to the boil and pour over the chocolate and butter. Stir with a wooden spoon until the chocolate and butter have melted and the glaze is smooth. While it is still warm, pour the glaze liberally over the prepared cake. Use a palette knife or the back of a metal spoon to spread the chocolate over the cake top and sides. Holding the rack with both hands gently tap it to allow the chocolate glaze to even itself and settle over the cake. Decorate with dark chocolate shards as shown in the techniques on page 147.

chocolate orange roulade

Chocolate and orange go together so well that this is an instant winner. It can be made in advance and filled prior to serving. Keep the orange cream well chilled so the filled roulade holds its shape. This recipe is rich and indulgent and forms a perfect centrepiece.

for the roulade

50g self raising flour

1 tsp baking powder

25g cocoa powder

50g ground almonds

5 large eggs

100g golden caster sugar, plus extra for turning the cake out

zest of 2 oranges

for the filling

2 x 250g tubs mascarpone

50g icing sugar

zest of 2 oranges and 2 tbsp juice

for the frosting

200g dark chocolate, broken into pieces

175g unsalted butter, softened

50g icing sugar

method

1 Heat the oven to 190°C (fan oven 170°C). Butter a 30cm x 40cm Swiss roll tin and line the base and sides with non-stick baking parchment.

2 Sift the self raising flour, baking powder and cocoa into a bowl and mix in the ground almonds. Put the eggs and caster sugar in a large mixing bowl and beat for 5–10 minutes using an electric hand whisk until pale and thick. The mixture should have trebled in volume and leave a trail when the beaters are lifted out. Fold the dry ingredients and orange zest into the egg mixture using a large metal spoon.

3 Pour the mixture into the prepared tin ensuring all the corners are filled and even. Bake for 12–15 minutes until firm to the touch. Meanwhile, soak a tea towel in cold water and ring out. Lay this on a clean work surface with a sheet of non-stick baking parchment on top. Sprinkle the parchment with golden caster sugar.

4 Once baked, remove the sponge from the oven and allow to cool for 1 minute before turning out on to the sugared paper. Peel away the baking paper in strips and with the short side facing you, roll the sponge up with the paper keeping the cold, wet tea towel on the outside. Set aside until completely cold.

5 To make the filling, beat the mascarpone and icing sugar with the fresh orange zest and juice. Unroll the roulade, discard the paper and spread the mascarpone mixture over the entire sponge. Roll up carefully as tight as possible and transfer to a serving plate.

6 To make the frosting, melt the chocolate in a heatproof bowl over a pan of simmering water. Allow to cool for 10 minutes. Beat the butter and icing sugar together until pale and smooth. Pour in the chocolate and stir thoroughly to combine. Set aside for 20 minutes to firm up slightly before spreading the frosting over the roulade with a palette knife.

to serve

The roulade can be made up to a day in advance. Take it out of the fridge at least 30 minutes before serving to allow the filling and icing to soften.

lemon and lime roulade

Roulades are deceptively easy to make and always look very impressive when served. This roulade combines the fresh zest of lemons and limes for a light, refreshing dessert – it can be made a day in advance and filled prior to serving.

for the roulade

30g butter, plus extra for greasing

115g plain flour, plus extra for dusting

4 eggs

115g golden caster sugar

zest of 2 lemons

zest of 2 limes

for the filling

200ml whipping cream

zest of 1 lemon

zest of 1 lime

6 tbsp lemon curd

to decorate

icing sugar

fresh edible flowers

method

1 Heat the oven to 180°C (fan oven 160°C). Butter a 40 x 30cm Swiss roll tin and line the base and sides with non-stick baking parchment. Dust lightly with flour and chill.

2 Melt the butter then set aside to cool. Place the eggs and sugar in a large mixing bowl and whisk until the mixture forms a thick trail (5 minutes), then briefly whisk in the lemon and lime zests. Sieve the flour into the mixture and gently fold in with a metal spoon. Pour in the cooled, melted butter and gently fold in until well mixed.

3 Scrape the mixture into the prepared tin and spread with a palette knife until it forms an even layer approximately 1cm thick. Bake in the oven for 6–8 minutes until just cooked.

4 Soak a tea towel in cold water and ring out. Lay this on a clean work surface with a sheet of non-stick baking parchment on top. Sprinkle the parchment with golden caster sugar. Invert the roulade on to the paper. Carefully roll the roulade up and leave aside.

5 To make the filling, whip the cream and fold in the zest of lemon and lime. Unroll the roulade and discard the paper. Spread the lemon curd and then the cream over the roulade and roll up tightly.

to serve

Heavily dust the top with sieved icing sugar and decorate with fresh edible flowers.

storage

The roulade can be made up to a day in advance.

tip

Alternatively serve the cake with fresh summer berries and lightly whipped fresh cream.

mango and passion-fruit pavlova roulade

Making a roulade from meringue can seem quite daunting, but it is much easier to handle than it may appear. The elasticity of the egg whites helps to roll the roulade and it has a lovely light, soft texture with a crisp outer crust.

for the roulade

3 large egg whites

175g golden caster sugar

1 level tsp cornflour

1 tsp malt vinegar

1 tsp vanilla extract

icing sugar, for dusting

for the filling

250g carton mascarpone

1 large ripe mango, peeled, stoned and finely chopped

148ml carton double cream

2 passion fruits, pulp only

to decorate

icing sugar

method

1 Heat the oven to 140°C (fan oven 130°C). Line a 33 x 23cm Swiss roll tin with non-stick baking parchment.

2 Beat the egg whites with an electric whisk until doubled in volume. Slowly whisk in the caster sugar until thick and shiny. Mix the cornflour, vinegar and vanilla extract, then whisk into the egg whites.

3 Spoon into the tin and level the surface carefully, avoiding knocking out too many air bubbles. Bake for 30 minutes until the meringue surface is just firm. Meanwhile make the filling: beat the mascarpone and stir in the finely chopped mango. Whip the double cream until thick then fold into the mango mix. Halve the passion fruit, scoop out the flesh and set aside.

4 Remove the meringue from the oven and cover with damp greaseproof paper for 10 minutes. Dust another sheet of greasproof paper with icing sugar. Discard the damp paper and turn the meringue out on to the icing-sugar dusted paper. Peel the paper away from the back of the meringue in strips.

5 Spread the meringue with the mango cream and drizzle over the passion fruit. Roll up the roulade from the short side using the paper to assist and carefully transfer to a serving plate.

to serve

Dust liberally with icing sugar to serve.

storage

The roulade can be made up to a day in advance.

vanilla pavlova with chocolate and marron

These individual meringue cases are filled with a deliciously nutty marron cream decorated with gentle shards of dark chocolate. They are ideal for a winter dinner party or autumnal cocktail party. The meringue can be made up to a week in advance and filled with the cream just before serving.

makes up to 20 individual meringues

for the meringue

3 medium egg whites

175g golden caster sugar

1 tsp cornflour

½ tsp vanilla extract

½ tsp white wine vinegar

150g white chocolate

for the filling

284ml plus 142ml carton double cream

2 small tins sweetened chestnut purée (crème de marron)

100g dark chocolate, grated

method

1 Heat the oven to 140°C (fan oven 120°C). Line 2 large baking sheets with non-stick baking paper. In a large bowl, whisk the egg whites until stiff. Gradually whisk in the sugar 1 tbsp at a time until the mixture is very stiff and shiny. Sift in the cornflour then, using a large metal spoon, fold in along with the vanilla extract and vinegar. Place large tablespoonfuls of meringue mixture on the parchment paper and gently flatten each one to 7.5cm diameter and make a light indent in each one.

2 Bake in the oven for 35–40 minutes until the meringue mixture is hard. Cool on a wire rack.

3 Melt the white chocolate and use a pastry brush to line each meringue case with white chocolate. Allow to set.

4 For the filling, whip the cream then fold in the sweetened chestnut purée.

5 With two dessertspoons, shape a oval quenelle of the filling and drop into the centre of each meringue; top with grated dark chocolate.

pistachio meringue gâteau

This impressive meringue gâteau combines three layers of soft, chewy, nutty meringue with seasonal berries and fresh cream. It cuts beautifully and is perfect for a dinner party at any time of the year.

for the meringue

125g shelled pistachios

5 large egg whites

300g golden caster sugar

1 tsp malt vinegar

1 tsp vanilla extract

for the red fruit compote

250g strawberries

250g raspberries

2 tbsp water

75g golden caster sugar

for the filling

568ml carton double cream

250g strawberries

250g raspberries

100g redcurrants

method

1 Heat the oven to 190°C (fan oven 170°C.) Line 3 x 20cm sandwich tins with non-stick baking parchment (alternatively draw 3 x 20cm circles on non-stick paper, and place the paper on baking sheets).

2 Place the pistachios on a baking sheet and bake in the centre of the oven for 10–15 minutes until golden brown. Allow to cool, then chop finely.

3 Place the egg whites in a clean, grease free bowl and whisk until stiff but not dry. Add the sugar gradually, whisking well after each addition. When the mixture is very stiff, add the vinegar and vanilla extract.

4 Fold in the chopped nuts using a metal spoon. Divide the mixture between the 3 tins (or paper circles) and level the tops with the back of the metal spoon – dragging the top of one meringue into interesting peaks. Bake in the oven for 30–35 minutes until firm to the touch.

5 Leave in the tins to cool completely then turn out on to a wire rack and remove the paper.

6 To make the red fruit compote, put the strawberries, raspberries, water and sugar in a pan. Bring to the boil then simmer for 20–25 minutes until reduced and the fruit has broken down. Allow to cool completely.

7 To fill the meringue gateau, whip the cream. Place the base meringue on a serving plate and spread over one third of the cream, drizzle 3 tbsp of the red fruit compote on top and one third of the fresh strawberries and raspberries; repeat with the second layer and finish with the third layer of meringue forming nice peaks. Spread with cream and fresh berries including the redcurrants. Serve the remaining red fruit compote in a separate dish on the side.

storage

The meringue can be made up to two weeks in advance and filled the day of serving.

cookies and pastries

cookies and pastries

Cookies and pastries are a fantastic addition to most parties. Themed, hand-decorated cookies can be served and eaten on the day or packaged in clear cellophane or organza bags and presented as gifts or place settings. For more elaborate table-centre decorations I have included a 'gingerbread house' using a traditional *Lebkuchen* recipe and the deliciously sweet traditional Persian sweetmeat *baklava*.

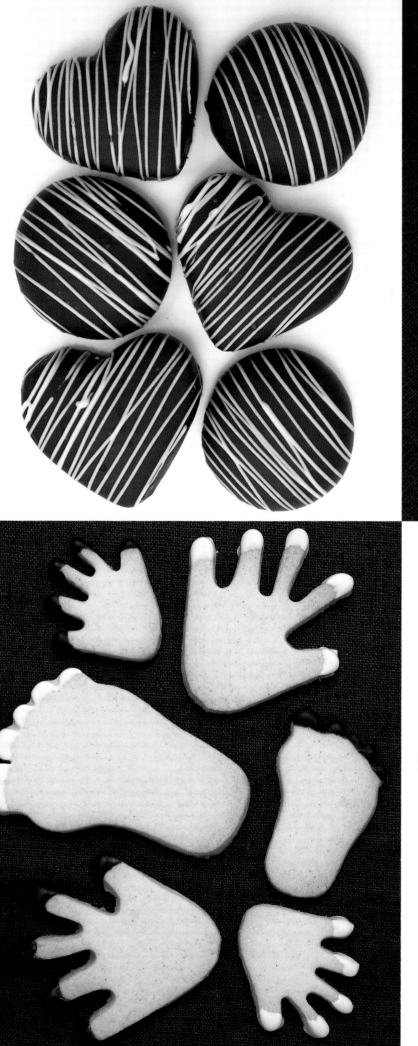

strawberry shortcake

The epitome of an English summer – conjuring up images of Wimbledon and cricket – these strawberry shortcakes are canapé-sized bakes, making them perfect for summer fêtes or buffet parties. Serve on a delicate cake stand accompanied by pink champagne or place three *fraises des bois* in a glass and top up with sparkling wine.

makes 32

for the shortcake
175g unsalted butter, softened
115g golden caster sugar
zest of 1 lemon
1 tsp vanilla extract
115g ground almonds
175g plain flour
flour, for dusting

for the filling
284ml tub double cream
250g little scarlet strawberry preserve
piping bag and fluted nozzle
400g *fraises des bois* or sliced strawberries
icing sugar, for dusting

method

1 Cream together the butter and sugar until light and fluffy. Stir in the lemon zest and vanilla extract. Add the ground almonds and flour and mix well to form a dough. Wrap the dough in cling film and chill for 30 minutes. Preheat the oven to 160°C (fan oven 140°C). Line 2 baking sheets with non-stick baking parchment.

2 On a lightly floured surface, roll the dough to a thickness of 5mm. Cut out 5cm rounds with a fluted pastry cutter. Lift on to the baking sheets with a palette knife. Bake in the oven for 12–15 minutes until lightly golden. Leave to cool for 2 minutes then transfer to a wire rack until cold.

3 For the filling, whip the cream until firm.

4 Place a teaspoon of the preserve on the base of half the shortcake rounds. Using a fluted nozzle, pipe swirls of cream on top and add a slice of fresh strawberry or 3 *fraises des bois*. Place a disc of shortcake on top at a slight angle and dust with icing sugar. Repeat with the remaining rounds.

flamingo cookies

Decorated cookies are a fabulous way to involve children with the cooking as the method is simple and the results instant. Here I have used flamingo cutters, but feel free to adapt for your own favourite cutter. For a more elaborate cookie that can be wrapped in a cellophane bag or boxed as a table setting or present, I have made flamingo cookies and decorated them with coloured royal icing.

makes 12 large cookies

for the cookies

200g unsalted butter, softened

200g golden caster sugar

1 medium free range egg, beaten

2 tsp pure vanilla bean paste

400g plain flour, plus extra for dusting

shaped cookie cutter or template cut out of card

to decorate

1 quantity royal icing (page 145)

piping bags

no. 1.5 nozzles

black, pink and yellow edible food colours

paintbrush

clear cellophane bags

ribbon

method

1 Preheat oven to 180°C (fan oven 160°C). Gently cream the butter and sugar together then add the beaten egg to combine. Stir in the vanilla bean paste. Gently fold in the flour and mix until the dough combines. Wrap the dough in cling film and chill for 30 minutes.

2 Lightly flour a work surface and roll the dough out to a thickness of 5mm. Stamp flamingo shapes out from the cookie dough and place well apart on a non-stick baking sheet.

3 Bake the cookies for 10 minutes until pale golden. Allow to cool slightly before transferring to a wire rack.

4 Fill a piping bag with a no. 1.5 nozzle and white royal icing. Pipe the outline of the flamingo. Remove 1 tbsp icing, colour black and transfer into a piping bag with no. 1.5 nozzle.

5 Thin the remainder of the icing with water to a flooding consistency. Colour three quarters pink, and one quarter yellow. Flood the pink body of the flamingo first using a paintbrush to reach all the corners and swirl a feather effect across the body. Allow to skin over before flooding the yellow legs and beak and finally piping the black legs, eye and tip of the beak.

6 Allow to set overnight before wrapping in cellophane bags and tying with a pretty ribbon.

hands and feet cookies

Children love to be involved in baking these, as they are quick and easy to make – not to mention fun and delicious as well! For a simple finish I have made vanilla and chocolate hands and feet and dipped the toes and fingers in melted chocolate.

makes 48 cookies

for the vanilla cookies

200g unsalted butter, softened

200g golden caster sugar

1 medium free range egg, beaten

400g plain flour, plus extra for dusting

2 tsp pure vanilla bean paste

for the chocolate cookies

replace 50g flour with 50g cocoa and omit the vanilla

to decorate

75g each white and dark chocolate, melted separately, for dipping the toes/fingers

method

1 Preheat oven to 180°C (fan oven 160°C). Gently cream the butter and sugar together then add the beaten egg to combine. Gently fold in the flour and vanilla paste and mix until the dough combines. Wrap the dough in cling film and chill for 30 minutes.

2 Lightly flour a work surface and roll the dough out to a thickness of 5mm. Use cutters or templates to cut out the hands and feet and place well apart on non-stick baking sheets.

3 Bake the cookies for 10 minutes until pale golden.

4 Allow to cool slightly before transferring to a wire rack. When cold, dip the toes and fingers in the melted chocolate and leave to set on non-stick baking paper.

tip

You needn't purchase expensive cookie cutters – trace a design on to card and cut out around each one for a variety of designs. Vary the designs to suit the occasion. Decorated teapots can look lovely served with afternoon tea.

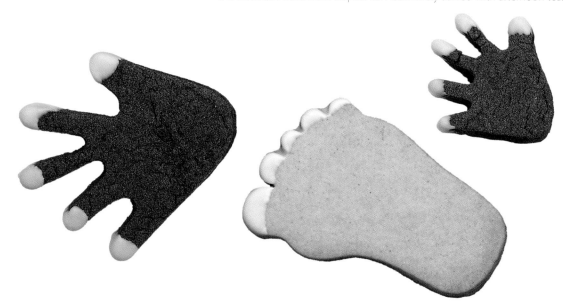

lebkuchen

One of the highlights of my year is visiting my sister in Munich for the annual Christmas markets in December. I can be guaranteed a biting wind, sufficiently potent *Gluhwein* and warm, freshly baked spiced *Lebkuchen*. Christmas has begun!

**makes 40 individual cookies
or 1 gingerbread house**

for the Lebkuchen
115g unsalted butter, softened
115g light muscovado sugar
1 medium egg, beaten
115g black treacle
400g self raising flour, plus extra
for dusting
1 tsp ground ginger
½ tsp ground cloves
½ tsp ground chilli

for covering and decorating
115g milk chocolate, melted
115g dark chocolate, melted
115g white chocolate, melted
piping bags
cocoa powder, for dusting

method

1 Cream together the butter and sugar until pale and fluffy. Beat in the egg and black treacle. Sift the flour, ginger, cloves and chilli into the bowl. Use a wooden spoon to draw all the ingredients together until well mixed and it forms a stiff paste. Knead gently on a lightly floured work surface then wrap in cling film and chill for 30 minutes. Preheat the oven to 180°C (fan oven 160°C). Line 2 baking sheets with non-stick baking parchment.

2 On a lightly floured surface, roll out half the dough to a thickness of 5mm. Cut out 5cm heart shapes with a pastry cutter. Lift on to the baking sheets with a palette knife. Divide the remaining dough into 20 pieces, roll into balls then place on the baking sheet. Flatten slightly with your fingers. Chill for a further 30 minutes.

3 Bake in the oven for 8–10 minutes. Transfer to a wire rack and allow to cool.

4 Melt and temper the chocolates (see page 147) separately in heatproof bowls over simmering water. Fill three small piping bags with 1 tbsp of each of the melted chocolates.

5 With the cookies on a wire rack and a piece of non-stick baking parchment underneath the rack, use a metal spoon to cover each cookie with melted chocolate. Tap the rack gently to smooth and remove excess chocolate. Repeat with the three different chocolates until all cookies are covered. (If the chocolate starts to set, return the bowl over the heat.)

6 Dust several of the cookies with cocoa powder. Snip the end off the piping bags while the chocolate is still warm and drizzle across the remaining cookies in a zig-zag design. Allow to cool and set before serving.

gingerbread house

The *Lebkuchen* recipe can be used to make individual cookies, covered in chocolate, or built into the most delightful gingerbread house – much easier than it looks and actually quite a lot of fun!

you will need

1 quantity Lebkuchen dough (page 127)

piping bags

2 quantities royal icing (page 145)

no. 1.5, 2, 3 and star nozzles

edible hologram glitter

25cm round cake board

red and green edible food colours

jelly bean sweets

50g white sugar paste

flower plunger-cutters

100g green sugar paste

1 metre x 15mm green ribbon

method

1 Following the recipe on page 127, roll out the dough to a large square sheet to a thickness of 5mm, and bake in the oven at the given temperature.

2 Allow to cool slightly then cut out the base, 2 sides, 2 ends, 2 roof panels and 2 pieces for the chimney with a large serrated knife, using the templates on pages 154–5.

3 Allow to cool completely. Fill a piping bag with white royal icing and snip the end. Pipe a thick line of icing along the base edge of one side panel and attach to the base. Repeat with the other side. Next take the end panels and pipe a thick line of icing as shown and attach to the base and sides. Pipe a thick line of icing along the top edge of the 2 side panels and fix the roof into position with a thick line of icing along the join at the top. Stick the 2 chimney pieces together with a little royal icing. Allow to set.

4 Using a piping bag filled with a star nozzle and white royal icing, pipe rows of stars along the centre line of the roof and down both sides to cover the roof. Place the chimney pieces in position and cover the top with white royal icing. Sprinkle the icing with edible hologram glitter. Allow to set.

5 Line a cake board with white icing and use a palette knife to texture a snow effect. Position the gingerbread house in the centre of the board and decorate. Use coloured icing to create windows and doors and surround with jelly bean sweets. Plunge flowers from the white sugar paste and fix these into position around the house. To make the trees, mould the green sugar paste into 3 cone shapes of different sizes. Snip around the cone with the end of a pair of small sharp scissors. Finish by fixing green ribbon around the base board.

storage
Keeps for 1 month.

nantucket ginger cookies

These hand-decorated ginger spiced cookies look very festive, tied with ribbon on the Christmas tree, served on a pretty plate, or presented in cellophane bags or smart ribboned boxes.

makes 24

for the cookies

115g unsalted butter, softened

115g soft light brown sugar

1 tsp vanilla extract

175g plain flour, plus extra for dusting

15g cocoa powder

2 tsp ground ginger

2 tbsp milk

for cutting, covering and decorating

7.5cm heart and star cookie cutters

large drinking straw

1 quantity royal icing, for piping (page 145)

red edible food colour

piping bags

no. 1.5 nozzles

1 quantity each white and red royal icing, for flooding (page 145)

gingham ribbon, 50cm for each cookie including bow

method

1 Preheat the oven to 190°C (fan oven 170°C). Line a baking sheet with non-stick baking parchment. Cream together the butter, sugar and vanilla extract until pale and fluffy. Sieve together the flour, cocoa and ginger. Work this in slowly to the creamed mixture adding a little milk to bind together.

2 Tip the dough on to a lightly floured surface and knead gently. Wrap the dough in cling film and chill for 30 minutes.

3 Roll out the dough to 7mm thick. Stamp out heart and star shapes using a 7.5cm cutter. Transfer to the baking sheet. Use the end of a large drinking straw to make a hole in the top of each cookie. Bake in the oven for 12–15 minutes until lightly golden. Leave on the baking sheets to cool then remove to a wire rack to cool completely.

4 Divide the royal icing into two bowls and colour one half with the red edible colour. Fill a piping bag with a no. 1.5 nozzle and white royal icing. Pipe the outline on half of the hearts and stars. Fill a second piping bag with white flooding icing and flood inside the lines. Repeat with the red icing on the other half of the cookies. Allow to set for 2 hours until a skin has formed on the biscuit.

5 Fill a piping bag with a no. 1.5 nozzle and red royal icing. Pipe a design in the centre of all the white cookies – freehand but using the templates on page 156 as a guide. Repeat with white royal icing on the red cookies. Allow to set overnight.

6 Make a bow from the gingham ribbon for each cookie. Tie a 30cm length of gingham ribbon through the hole, fix the ribbon into position with royal icing and hang from the tree or serve on a pretty plate.

4

5

baklava

This is a traditional Persian sweetmeat served to celebrate the first official day of spring – 21st March. The layers of thin pastry are interspersed with toasted pistachios and drenched in a delicious sweet syrup infused with rose water. Baklava is perfect served after dinner with coffee or fresh mint tea.

for the pastry

350g finely chopped toasted pistachios

150g icing sugar

150g unsalted butter, melted

450g filo pastry

for the syrup

300g granulated sugar

200ml water

2 tbsp rose water

method

1 Make the syrup. Place the sugar and water for the syrup in a saucepan, bring to the boil then reduce the heat and simmer for 10 minutes, until thickened. Stir in the rose water and set aside.

2 Mix together the nuts and icing sugar. Preheat the oven to 160°C (fan oven 140°C). Brush a baking tin 18 x 27.5 x 5cm with butter and line the base with non-stick baking parchment.

3 Taking one sheet of filo pastry at a time, and keeping the remainder covered with a damp cloth, brush with melted butter and lay on the bottom of the tin. Repeat with 5 layers of pastry. Spread half the nut mixture over and press down with the back of a spoon.

4 Add another 5 layers of pastry, brush with butter and spoon over the remaining nuts. Finish with 5 layers of pastry. Cut the baklava into strips then diamonds and pour the remaining butter over the top. Bake in the oven for 20 minutes, then increase the temperature to 200°C (fan oven 180°C) and bake for a further 15 minutes until rich golden in colour and well risen.

5 Remove from the oven and drizzle the syrup over the baklava. Allow to cool in the tin, then remove, gently tease the baklava apart with a sharp knife and serve.

techniques

techniques In this section you will find the techniques needed to cover, ice, decorate and stack my *Fantastic Party Cakes*. I have included instructions for making royal icing, flooding icing and fondant as well as how to colour sugar paste and make sugar decorations. I show you how to temper chocolate before using it to create chocolate decorations, scrolls and fans. Refer to these pages for the cakes in this book or use them for inspiration when creating your own designs.

buttercream

Buttercream is a combination of softened unsalted butter and icing sugar. The basic mixture can be combined with other flavours: these orange, lemon curd, espresso and chocolate ganache versions are particularly good. For lime and coconut see page 80.

yields 750g

ingredients

250g unsalted butter, softened

500g icing sugar

1 tsp vanilla extract

Beat the softened butter for 2 minutes using an electric whisk. Sieve in the icing sugar and beat slowly at first. Add the vanilla extract then, with the whisk on full speed, whip until the buttercream is very light and fluffy.

fresh orange buttercream

Stir the grated zest of 2 fresh oranges and 4 tbsp juice into 1 quantity of buttercream. This buttercream works equally well layered between a vanilla cake or chocolate-based cake.

lemon curd buttercream

This buttercream is ideal as an alternative to fresh cream or mascarpone for filling the Vanilla cake (page 83) as it is shelf stable and suitable for use where the cake is to be covered in chocolate or marzipan and icing Simply stir 275g of lemon curd into 1 quantity of buttercream.

espresso buttercream

I particularly like this espresso buttercream as it is very indulgent. Use to top the Chocolate and Almond cake (page 90) or sandwich in the Chocca Mocca Pecan cake (page 95). Pour 200ml freshly boiled water on to 100g of fresh ground coffee and allow to steep for 5 minutes. Strain the espresso and leave to cool slightly. Stir into 1 quantity of buttercream mixture until you have the desired intensity of flavour.

chocolate ganache buttercream

Chocolate ganache is a blend of boiled cream and chocolate. It has a smooth, rich, velvety texture that literally melts in the mouth. Mixed with buttercream it becomes a wonderfully decadent filling or frosting.

ingredients

175g dark chocolate (70% cocoa solids), broken into pieces

125g fresh double cream

1 quantity of buttercream

Place the chocolate pieces in a clean dry bowl. Bring the cream to the boil, remove from the heat and pour over the chocolate. Stir with a wooden spoon until the chocolate is melted and the ganache is smooth and glossy. Allow the chocolate ganache to cool for 15 minutes before beating it into the buttercream. Store any excess buttercream in the refrigerator for up to 2 weeks.

cutting out small cakes

Individual cakes are stamped or cut out of a single larger tier. There will be wastage when cutting out round cakes – save this to create truffles or as the base for a delicious trifle. A 20cm square single layer cake will yield 16 x 5cm individual cakes or 25 x 4cm canapé cakes. If using buttercream, split the layer of cake horizontally and spread with buttercream. Replace the top and use a round cutter to stamp out the round cakes.

Cut rounds of cake using a 4cm cutter.

Cut a 20cm square cake into 20 slices, each measuring 5 x 4cm. Use a ruler as a guide or cut a 5cm template in thick card.

marzipan

One question I am often asked is: 'Do I have to use marzipan?' Some seem to love, and some loathe, this luxurious almond paste. In fact, marzipan plays a threefold role as a covering for a cake: firstly, it protects the cake, locking in moisture; secondly, it adds form and stability – especially if the cake is for a tiered cake; thirdly, it provides a good clean base for the icing, which prevents the colour of the cake bleeding through. For multi-tiered cakes I recommend it as essential; however, you could cover a single-tier cake with a double layer of sugar paste instead if you wish.

covering a large cake with marzipan

you will need

cake

thin board the same size as the cake

pastry brush

boiled, sieved apricot jam

marzipan

icing sugar

rolling pin

smoother

turntable or bowl

sharp knife

1 Place the cooled, baked cake upside down on a thin cake board the same size as the cake and brush liberally with boiled, sieved apricot jam. Knead the marzipan until smooth and pliable. Dust the work surface lightly with icing sugar and roll the marzipan evenly into a size large enough to cover the top and sides of the cake, allowing for surplus (use string to measure). The marzipan should be approximately 5mm thick. Carefully lift the marzipan on to the cake.

2 Smooth the top and sides of the cake using your hands and a smoother. Trim off the majority of the excess marzipan.

3 Lift the cake on to a turntable or upturned bowl and neatly trim the final excess marzipan using a sharp knife and keeping it flush with the bottom of the board.

TIP – alternatively, for those who loathe marzipan, cover the cakes with an initial layer of white chocolate plastique prior to being covered with sugar paste.

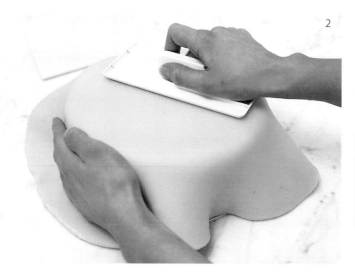

1

2

3

covering an individual round cake with marzipan

Individual cakes need to be perfectly covered with marzipan and sugar paste before they are decorated. This is a skilled process, which requires practice and patience. All individual cakes are cut from one large cake: rounds are stamped out with a cutter and square cakes are cut with a sharp knife. Whether the cakes are square or round, covered with marzipan and sugar paste or chocolate plastique, the techniques are very similar.

1

1 Brush the sides and top of the cakes with boiled, slightly cooled apricot jam.

2 Roll out the marzipan to a thickness of 3–4mm and cut into squares approximately 15 x 15cm. Place a square over each cake and press down all the way round.

3 Use a slightly larger cutter (5cm for canapé size or 6cm for individual size) carefully position over the marzipanned cake and stamp out. Remove the excess marzipan. Use 2 straight edge smoothers together to flatten the top and neaten the sides and base edge.

2   3

petal paste and modelling paste

Ready-made petal paste or modelling paste is available from most cake decorating stores. It dries harder and can be rolled more thinly than sugar paste, allowing for larger models or finer flowers. It will keep for up to 1 month tightly wrapped in cling film, in an airtight container.

yields 450g

2 tsp powdered gelatine

450g icing sugar, sieved

3 tsp gum tragacanth

2 tsp liquid glucose

2 tsp white fat

1 egg white

1 Soak the gelatine in 5 tsp cold water for 30 minutes. Meanwhile heat the icing sugar and gum tragacanth in a bowl over a saucepan of hot water.

2 Dissolve the liquid glucose, fat and gelatine over a low heat.

3 Beat the sugar mixture in an electric mixer at low speed. Add the glucose mixture and egg white. Turn to maximum speed and beat for 15 minutes.

sugar paste

Sugar paste is a wonderful invention. Rolled out like marzipan and smoothed over the cake, this sweet paste creates a fast, clean, smooth finish with gently curved edges. It is soft and pliable to apply; sets firm but not rock hard; cuts beautifully and has a shelf life of one year. However, it does not like to get wet – moisture will dissolve the sugar leaving craters, so keep all utensils clean and thoroughly dry.

covering a large cake with sugar paste

1 Brush the thick baseboard with cooled boiled water. Dust the work surface lightly with icing sugar (too much will dry the sugar paste) and knead the sugar paste until smooth and pliable. Evenly roll the paste to the correct size – large enough to cover the baseboard and approximately 3mm thick. Carefully place the icing over the board and use a smoother to finish. Holding the board in one hand, use a sharp knife to cut away the excess, keeping the knife flush with the side of the board. Set aside to set (ideally overnight).

2 Brush the marzipan-covered cake with brandy or cooled boiled water. This acts as a good antiseptic seal between the marzipan and sugar paste as well as being an adhesive.

3 Dust the work surface lightly with icing sugar and knead the sugar paste until smooth and pliable. Evenly roll the sugar paste into a size large enough to cover the top and sides of the cake, allowing for surplus (use string to measure). It should be approximately 5mm thick. Carefully lift the sugar paste on to the marzipan-covered cake.

4 Smooth the top and sides with your hands, carefully pressing the sugar paste against the cake. Be careful not to drag the icing down the sides of the cake as this will cause it to crack and tear.

5 Use a smoother to give the cake a professional, clean finish and prick any air bubbles with a pin. Trim most of the excess sugar paste away from the cake.

6 Lift the cake on to a turntable or upturned bowl and neatly trim away all the excess sugar paste using a sharp knife, keeping the knife flush with the bottom of the board. Slide a palette knife carefully underneath the cake and board and lift from underneath using both hands. Put a dab of royal icing on the pre-lined baseboard and carefully set the cake in position on top.

you will need

marzipan-covered cake placed on a thin board of the same size

pastry brush

thick board 7.5cm larger than the cake

icing sugar

sugar paste

rolling pin

smoother

sharp knife

brandy or cooled boiled water

turntable or bowl

palette knife

small quantity of royal icing

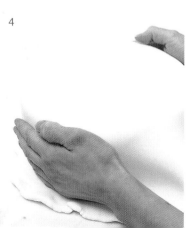

1 2

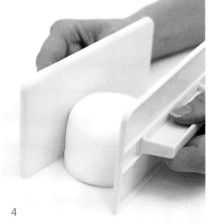

3 4

covering an individual round cake with sugar paste

Individual cakes are covered with a top coat of sugar paste once they have been covered either with a layer of marzipan or white chocolate plastique (for those who dislike marzipan) This will set firm overnight into allow handling and additional decoration.

1 Brush the marzipan-covered individual cake with brandy or cooled boiled water to help the sugar paste adhere.

2 Roll out the sugar paste to a thickness of 3–4mm and cut into squares approximately 20 x 20cm. Place a square over each cake and press down all the way round.

3 Use a slightly larger cutter (6cm for canapé size or 7.5cm for individual size), carefully position over the iced cake and stamp out. Remove the excess sugar paste.

4 Use 2 straight edge smoothers together to flatten the top and neaten the sides and base edge.

colouring sugar paste

Commercially coloured sugar paste is available to purchase, which can be helpful for covering a number of individual cakes or a larger tiered cake. However, for smaller quantities or more control over the exact colour it is simple to colour your own.

1

2

3

1 Knead a ball of white sugar paste on a clean surface lightly dusted with icing sugar. Edible colours specifically formulated for sugar craft are more concentrated and come as a paste. Insert a wooden cocktail stick or washable plastic dowelling rod into the colour paste. Drag it across the top of the sugar paste as shown.

2 Gently knead the paste until the colour is uniform throughout.

3 Test this by cutting the paste cleanly through the centre.

TIP – try not to use too much icing sugar as this will dry the paste out. If the paste begins to show signs of cracking, work a little white fat into the paste. Add enough edible colouring paste to create the desired intensity of colour.

TIP – for very dark colours or if colouring a number of different pastes, wear disposable gloves to avoid colouring your hands.

fondant

Fondant powder is available commercially – composed of icing sugar and glucose powder. Use 10ml water per 100g fondant powder and allow 75g icing per individual cake. Spoon it over each cake or carefully invert each cake and dip into the prepared fondant using a dipping fork.

covering a cake with fondant

1 Measure the fondant powder into a large bowl. Make a well in the centre and measure in the cooled boiled water.

2 Mix the fondant with a wooden spoon to a paste. This is the point to colour the fondant if desired.

3 Use a small amount of colour on the end of a cocktail stick. Blend with a wooden spoon.

4 Warm the fondant either over a pan of simmering water or for a brief time in a microwave. The fondant should be warmed to blood temperature (37°C) so it is just warm to the touch. The fondant should be less viscous at this stage. Use a large spoon and place the cake on a wire rack over a sheet of non-stick baking parchment. Carefully pour the fondant over the cake, using the back of the spoon to encourage it down the sides until they are fully covered.

5 Carefully remove the covered cake with a palette knife.

6 Position in a pretty paper case. Gather the sides around the cake and hold in position either with a length of tied ribbon or an elastic band until the icing has set firm.

2

3

4

5

6

royal icing

Royal icing is used for adding hand decoration to cakes, or thinned for flooding run-outs. Once made, royal icing will keep fresh in an airtight container for up to 7 days. It will separate if left for longer than 24 hours and should be rewhisked before using.

yields 400g

ingredients

1 medium egg white

350g icing sugar, sieved

juice of ½ lemon, strained

Place the egg white into a clean, grease-free bowl and whisk until it forms very soft peaks. Add the icing sugar and whisk slowly at first until all the sugar is incorporated, then on full speed for 1 minute. Add the lemon juice and whisk for another minute.

flooding icing

Flooding icing is used to fill the royal iced outlines for making run-outs. I have used this technique in several recipes including the decoration on the sugar paste discs for Coconut Butterflies on page 27.

Thin the royal icing down with drops of egg white or water. Egg white will make the finished run-out stronger but the icing may take longer to dry. Thinning the icing with water will enable it to dry quicker but it will be less strong. Add additional liquid a drop at a time to the royal icing and stir gently. Do not beat the icing as you will incorporate too much air and bubbles will appear in the run-outs. To judge the amount of water to add, swirl a knife in the bowl and count steadily to 10 as the ripples subside.

ingredients

1 quantity of royal icing

egg white or water

food colouring

using flooding icing to make a butterfly

This technique is used to decorate Sugar Candy (page 67).

1 Trace a selection of butterfly designs (see page 152) on to tracing paper and fix a piece of waxed paper over the top, shiny side up, holding both in position with masking tape. Using a no. 1.5 nozzle and white royal icing, pipe the outline.

2 Separate the flooding icing into 3 bowls, colour one yellow and one green, leaving one white. Fill 3 piping bags with the icing and flood the butterflies, making some with each colour. Use a small damp paintbrush to pull the icing to fill all the corners.

3 While the icing is still wet, add detail with a contrast colour inside the wings and drag with a cocktail stick to form patterns. Allow to set for 15 minutes then flood the lower wings. Leave the iced butterfly wings overnight to dry.

4 Peel the butterfly wings from the waxed paper. Fill a piping bag with a no. 3 nozzle and reserved royal icing. Pipe a head and body on to clean waxed paper and then attach wings on to the iced body at an angle, supporting each one with a small piece of sponge (or cotton wool). Insert 2 stamens for antennae. Leave to dry overnight. When dry attach the butterflies to the cake using a small amount of royal icing.

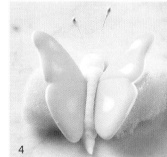

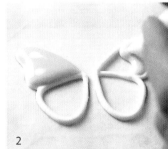

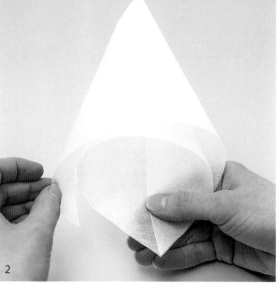

making a piping bag

Piping bags are made from triangles of non-stick baking paper. The larger the triangle, the larger the piping bag. I like to make various sizes – smaller ones for flooding lots of different colours and larger ones for piping single colours on to a number of tiers.

1 Fold a 30–45cm square of greaseproof paper in half diagonally to make 2 triangles and cut the paper in half along the crease. Place the paper on the table with the tip of the triangle facing you and bring the underside of the left point to the right of centre and hold with your thumb and forefinger.

2 Bring the right hand point up, over and round to the back to meet the centre.

3 Carefully fold the corner of the paper over to secure the bag, as shown.

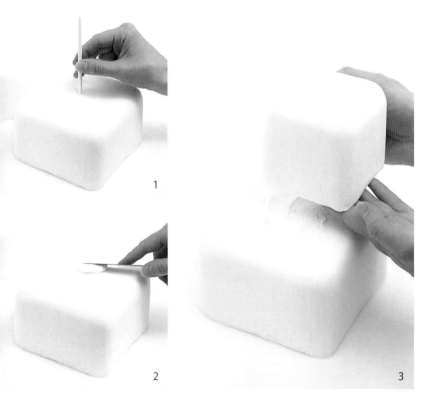

stacking tiers

Covered 5cm cakes can be stacked directly on to a larger tier without the need for a base board or dowelling rods. For all cakes 7.5cm or larger being stacked, they should first be covered on a board the same size as the cake, and the base tier should be dowelled to prevent the tiers collapsing or sinking.

1 Insert a dowelling rod into the centre of the base cake. Use a pencil to mark the point on the dowelling rod which is level with the top of the cake. Remove the dowelling rod. Line this dowelling rod up with 4 others and mark them all level with the guide mark. Cut the dowelling rods cleanly at the mark and check they are all the same length. Re-insert the central dowelling rod and 4 others around the sides, spread out but keeping within the dimensions of the upper tier.

2 Smear a small amount of royal icing on the top of the base cake.

3 Carefully lift the top tier into position. Slide the cake carefully until it is positioned centrally or purposely offset.

chocolate

I like to cover individual cakes with pure melted chocolate. The taste and finish is a clean, crisp chocolate with all the appeal of a decadent chocolate truffle. In order to work effectively with melted chocolate, it must first be tempered (or pre-crystallized) to achieve the shine, correct melting properties and stability required. Most importantly, tempering will prevent blooming (unsightly white streaks in the chocolate as it resets).

tempering chocolate

1 Break the chocolate into small pieces and place in a large clean bowl over a pan of simmering water. (Do not boil – if water or steam comes into contact with the chocolate, it will turn into a solid block. Water and chocolate do not mix!) Stir the chocolate while melting to ensure even heating but try to avoid creating air bubbles. Heat chocolate to 45°C.

2 Replace the hot water with cold water and stir continuously until the chocolate cools to 27°C. Occasionally it may be necessary to add additional cool water underneath the bowl.

3 Replace the cold water with warm water and raise the temperature of the chocolate to between 31°C and 32°C for dark chocolate, 30°C and 31°C for milk chocolate and 28°C and 29°C for white chocolate. Maintain the appropriate temperature while dipping. If the chocolate cools or warms outside of these temperatures, you will need to repeat the tempering process.

4 Test the temper of the chocolate before starting to dip. This can be done by spreading a small amount on to aluminium foil and allowing it to cool. It should be smooth and shiny with no dull or wet areas. Streaks may indicate poor temper or a lack of mixing. If the results are unsatisfactory, you will need to retemper the chocolate before proceeding.

making chocolate decorations

These are made from sheets of tempered chocolate and can be prepared in advance, then stored in an airtight container for up to 3 months. Use them to add the finishing decorations on any number of cakes, such as Marbled Chocolate Truffles (page 14).

1 **Chocolate scrolls** Spread the freshly tempered chocolate on to a clean marble slab or stainless steel baking tray to a thickness of 2mm. Using a specialized chocolate scraper, carefully push the scraper along the right hand edge of the chocolate as it begins to set, making a strip about 2cm wide and about 5cm long, until the chocolate has curled around twice. For chocolate shards as used on the Chocolate Strawberry Torte (page 106), allow the chocolate to set firm. Use this same technique to gather shards as the chocolate will be too hard to curl over itself.

2 **Chocolate fans** A similar technique to the scrolls – spread the tempered chocolate out as before. Once the chocolate begins to set, use the scraper along the right-hand side of the chocolate holding your finger along the edge of the scraper and chocolate as shown.

3 **Chocolate curls** Pour the freshly tempered chocolate into a small plastic container to a thickness of at least 1cm. Allow to set completely. Holding the block of chocolate in one hand, carefully pull a vegetable peeler across the chocolate to create the chocolate curls.

1

2

3

chocolate plastique

Chocolate plastique is a combination of pure chocolate with a sugar stock syrup – effectively glucose – which makes chocolate malleable, enabling you to roll it out to cover a cake or hand mould it to create the fans, roses and leaves used in many of the designs shown here. It has all the taste of chocolate, but with the texture of sugar paste and gives a smooth, firm finish to a cake. You can use chocolate plastique to cover a cake in exactly the same way as you would marzipan and sugar paste. To make milk chocolate plastique, knead together dark and white chocolate plastique.

plastique stock syrup

yields 450ml

ingredients

250ml water

140g caster sugar

85g glucose syrup

Place all the ingredients in a saucepan and bring to the boil. Remove from the heat and leave to cool. This recipe will provide slightly more than necessary to create the white chocolate plastique recipe below.

white chocolate plastique

yields 2¹⁄₂kg

ingredients

1.75kg white chocolate, broken into pieces

115g cocoa butter

400g glucose syrup

300ml stock syrup

1 Melt the chocolate in a microwave or place it in a clean, heat-resistant bowl over a saucepan of simmering water. Melt the cocoa butter in a microwave or place it in a clean, heat-resistant bowl over a saucepan of simmering water. (It is important to melt the cocoa butter and chocolate separately as they melt at different rates and both need to be melted for the recipe to work.) Mix the chocolate and cocoa butter together and stir well. Measure the glucose syrup and stock syrup together and warm slightly in the microwave. (This allows all the ingredients to be at a similar temperature for the final mix.)

2 Pour chocolate over glucose and stock syrups and mix well with a wooden spoon until smooth. Transfer the mixture into a clean large freezer bag and leave overnight at room temperature to set.

3 When ready to use, knead the chocolate plastique until smooth and pliable. Roll out on a work surface lightly dusted with icing sugar.

dark chocolate plastique

This paste is quite firm and chewy. Use this recipe for making hand moulded roses, lilies and other decorations but mix it 1:1 with white sugar paste for covering cakes.

Melt the chocolate in a microwave or place it in a clean, heat-resistant bowl over a pan of simmering water. Heat to 43°C. Heat the glucose syrup separately to the same temperature. Pour the syrup into the melted chocolate and stir with a wooden spoon until thoroughly combined. Allow to cool completely. Transfer the mixture into a clean large freezer bag and leave overnight at room temperature to set. To use, peel away the bag and knead the chocolate until smooth and pliable.

yields 2.25kg

you will need

1.25kg dark chocolate (55% maximum cocoa solids), broken into pieces

1kg glucose syrup

covering an individual square cake with chocolate plastique

Individual cakes can be covered with white chocolate plastique with a final coat of either sugar paste, or white or dark chocolate plastique. Cut the cake into squares using a ruler and a sharp knife as shown on page 139. Cut the individual cakes into 5cm squares, or canapé size 4cm squares. Brush the sides and top of the cakes with boiled, slightly cooled apricot jam.

1 Roll out the chocolate plastique to a thickness of 2–3mm and cut into squares approximately 15 x 15cm. Place a square over each cake and press down all the way round.

2 Square the sides using 2 straight-edge smoothers.

3 Trim the excess paste with a sharp knife. Use the smoothers again to flatten the top and neaten the sides and base edge. Repeat with the top coat which can be dark or white chocolate plastique or sugar paste.

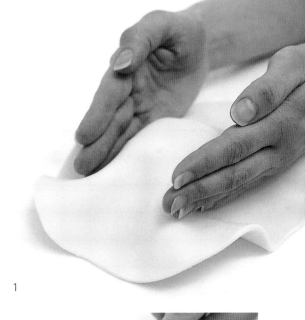

1

2

3

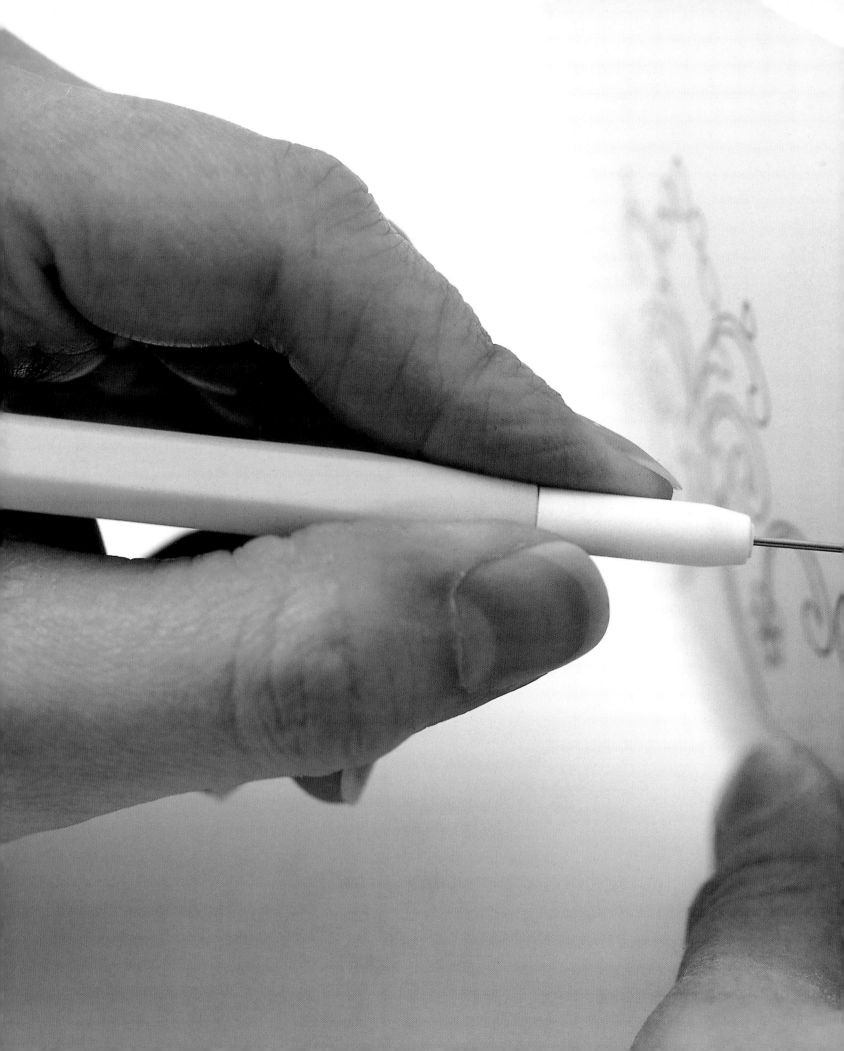

templates

bugs and butterflies

see page 28

bollywood

see page 22

coconut butterflies

see page 27

bunny building block

see page 71

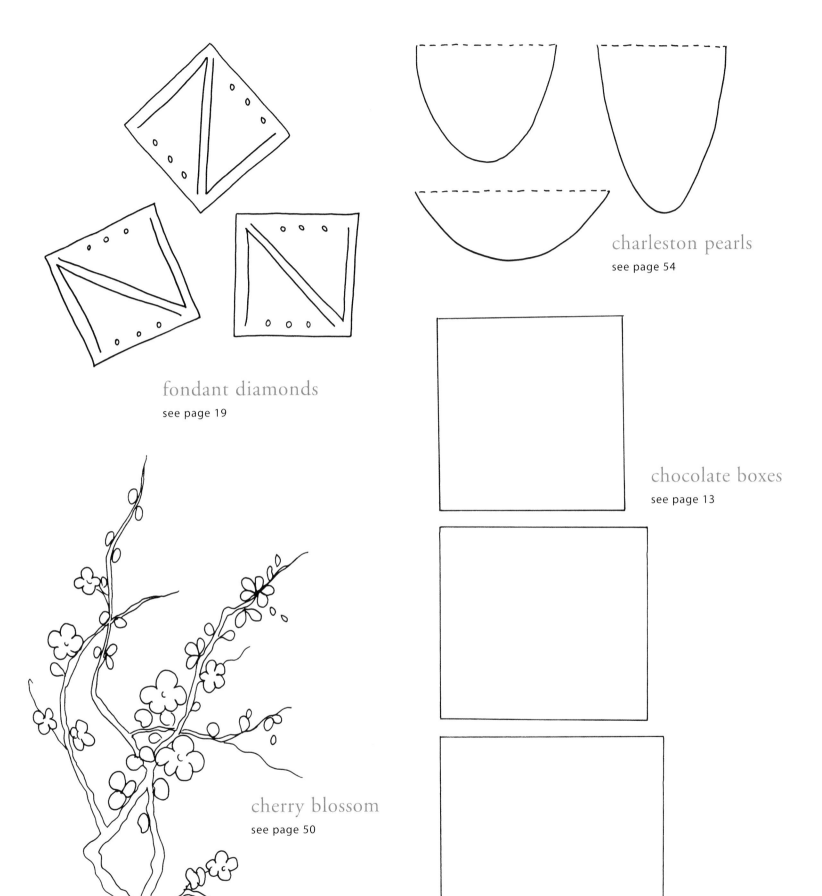

fondant diamonds

see page 19

charleston pearls

see page 54

chocolate boxes

see page 13

cherry blossom

see page 50

little venice lace™

see page 53

gingerbread house

roof panel (make 2)

see page 128

christmas canapé collection

see page 30

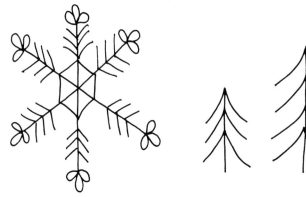

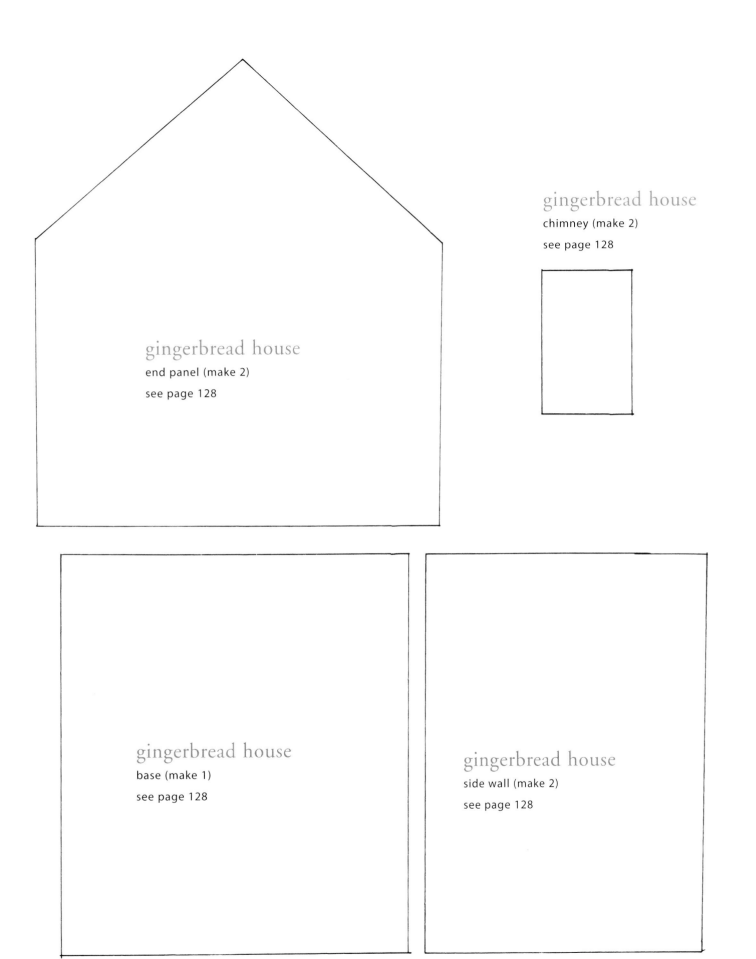

gingerbread house

end panel (make 2)

see page 128

gingerbread house

chimney (make 2)

see page 128

gingerbread house

base (make 1)

see page 128

gingerbread house

side wall (make 2)

see page 128

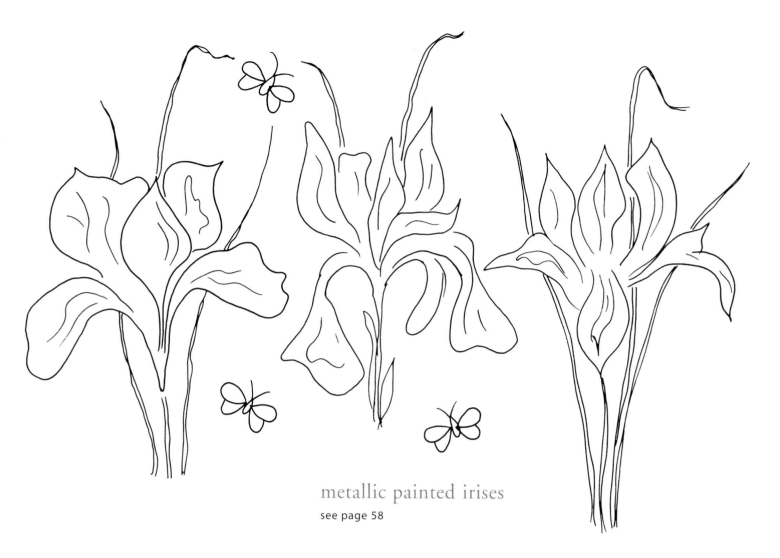

metallic painted irises
see page 58

monochrome lace

see page 20

nantucket ginger cookies

see page 130

santa star

see page 74

santa star

see page 74

santa star

see page 74

useful addresses

cake decorating supplies

Continental Chef Supplies
The Courtyard
South Hetton Industrial Estate
South Hetton
County Durham
DH6 2UZ
Tel 0808 100 1777
www.chefs.net

Divertimenti
Tel 0870 129 5027
www.divertimenti.co.uk

Lakeland
www.lakelandlimited.com

Little Venice Cake Company
15 Manchester Mews
Marylebone
London
W1U 2DX
Tel 020 7486 5252
www.LVCC.co.uk

Squires Shop
Squires House
3 Waverley Lane
Farnham, Surrey
GU9 8BB
Tel 0845 225 5671
www.squires-shop.com

Sugar Shack
87 Burntoak Broadway
Burntoak, Middlesex
HA8 5EP
Tel 0800 597 5097
www.sugarshack.co.uk

Surbiton Art and Sugarcraft
140 Hook Road
Surbiton, Surrey
KT6 5BZ
Tel 020 8391 4664
www.surbitonart.co.uk

florists

Neil Birks
5 Grosvenor Cottages
Eaton Terrace
London
SW1W 8HA
Tel 020 7259 9746 / 07770 881323
Email: neil@nbflowers.co.uk
www.nbflowers.co.uk

Rob Van Helden Floral Design Ltd.
8 Tun Yard
Peardon Street
London
SW8 3HT
Tel 020 7720 6774
www.rvhfloraldesign.com

Simon Lycett
30 Charter House Works
Eltringham Street
London
SW18 1TD
Tel 020 8874 1040
Email: enquiries@simonlycett.co.uk
www.simonlycett.co.uk

Paula Pryke
The Flower House
Cynthia Street
London
N1 9JF
Tel 020 7837 7336
ww.paula-pryke-flowers.com

Paul Thomas
The Greenery
4 Shepherd Street
London
W1J 7JD
Tel 020 7499 6889
www.paulthomasflowers.co.uk

cookie cutters

www.coppergifts.com

ribbons

Barnett Lawson (Trimmings) Ltd
16–17 Little Portland Street
London
W1W 8NE
Tel 020 7636 8591
www.bltrimmings.com

VV Rouleaux
102 Marylebone Lane
London
W1U 2QD
Tel 020 7224 5179
Also stores in Sloane Street,
Glasgow and Newcastle –
www.vvrouleaux.com

wedding planners

Siobhan Craven-Robins
70 Gun Place
86 Wapping Lane
London
E1W 2RX
Tel 020 7481 4338

Deborah Dwek Weddings
Deborah Dwek Limited
9 Hayward Road
London
N20 0HA
Tel 020 8446 9501 / 07941 660763
Email debbie.dwek@lineone.net
www.deborahdwekweddings.co.uk

Kathryn Lloyd Wedding Design
152 Grosvenor Road
London
SW1V 3JL
Tel / Fax 020 7828 5535
www.kathrynlloyd.co.uk

event planners

The Admirable Crichton
Unit 5 Camberwell Trading Estate
Denmark Road
London
SE5 9LB
Tel 020 7326 3800
www.admirable-crichton.co.uk

Bentley's Entertainments
7 Square Rigger Row
Plantation Wharf
London
SW11 3TZ
Tel 020 7223 7900

Party Planners
56 Ladbroke Grove
London
W11 2PB
Tel 020 7229 9666

Smith and Niemierko
Floor 6
456–458 The Strand
London
WC2R 0DZ
Tel 0870 990 3978
www.smithniemierko.com

Wedding Bible Company Limited
Old Barn
14 The Green
Drayton, Oxon
OX14 4HZ
Tel 01235 532 719
Mobile 07885 461 866
Email
sarah.haywood@weddingbible.co.uk

index

acknowledgements

Fantastic Party Cakes for Fantastic Party People – many of whom I would like to thank for all their hard work, patience and support in the preparation of this book, and in the sampling of this collection of mouthwatering cakes, puddings and sweet treats.

Thank you to my talented team at Little Venice Cake Company – especially Alison Thompson – another of my fine pastry chefs now back in Australia! – who so ably assisted with the Fluffy Desserts and chocolate work. Thank you to Christine Lee for your constant banter and intricate hand decorating skills and our future bride Megan Whelan for all your support. Come back soon Debbie who is on maternity leave. Congratulations to our newlyweds Rosie and Dan Shorten and welcome to our new boy in the kitchen – Colin Chih.

It was lovely to get the A Team together again to work on this book – I am indebted to Jacqui Small for the opportunity to indulge in more cakes; Rizzoli in New York for their enthusiasm; the ever so talented design team of Maggie Town and Beverly Price, for their art direction and design, and putting in many long hours; Janine Hosegood for her stunning photography and patience – and lunch everyday! (thanks, too, to Ralph and Max!); to the very pregnant, newly married (congratulations on both counts!) Kate John, also Judith Hannam and Madeline Weston for editing *Fantastic Party Cakes*.

I would also like to thank my parents – Celia and Ralph – your support is appreciated more than you can know.

Thank you to Katie Ackland Snow – for being such a super nanny to my wonderful boys and allowing me to juggle being a working mother.